I0410754

THE LONG ARM OF CHINA: GLOBAL EFFORTS TO SILENCE CRITICS FROM TIANANMEN TO TODAY

HEARING

BEFORE THE

CONGRESSIONAL-EXECUTIVE COMMISSION ON CHINA

ONE HUNDRED FOURTEENTH CONGRESS

SECOND SESSION

MAY 24, 2016

Printed for the use of the Congressional-Executive Commission on China

Available via the World Wide Web: http://www.cecc.gov

U.S. GOVERNMENT PUBLISHING OFFICE

20–804 PDF   WASHINGTON : 2016

For sale by the Superintendent of Documents, U.S. Government Publishing Office
Internet: bookstore.gpo.gov   Phone: toll free (866) 512–1800; DC area (202) 512–1800
Fax: (202) 512–2104   Mail: Stop IDCC, Washington, DC 20402–0001

CONGRESSIONAL-EXECUTIVE COMMISSION ON CHINA

LEGISLATIVE BRANCH COMMISSIONERS

House

CHRIS SMITH, New Jersey, *Chairman*
ROBERT PITTENGER, North Carolina
TRENT FRANKS, Arizona
RANDY HULTGREN, Illinois
DIANE BLACK, Tennessee
TIM WALZ, Minnesota
MARCY KAPTUR, Ohio
MICHAEL HONDA, California
TED LIEU, California

Senate

MARCO RUBIO, Florida, *Cochairman*
TOM COTTON, Arkansas
STEVE DAINES, Montana
JAMES LANKFORD, Oklahoma
BEN SASSE, Nebraska
DIANNE FEINSTEIN, California
JEFF MERKLEY, Oregon
GARY PETERS, Michigan

EXECUTIVE BRANCH COMMISSIONERS

CHRISTOPHER P. LU, Department of Labor
SARAH SEWALL, Department of State
STEFAN M. SELIG, Department of Commerce
DANIEL R. RUSSEL, Department of State
TOM MALINOWSKI, Department of State

PAUL B. PROTIC, *Staff Director*
ELYSE B. ANDERSON, *Deputy Staff Director*

(II)

CONTENTS

THE LONG ARM OF CHINA: GLOBAL EFFORTS TO SILENCE CRITICS FROM TIANANMEN TO TODAY

TUESDAY, MAY 24, 2016

Congressional-Executive
Commission on China,
Washington, DC.

The hearing was convened, pursuant to notice, at 12:05 p.m., in Room HVC–210, Capitol Visitor Center, Hon. Christopher Smith, Chairman, presiding.

Also Present: Senator Rubio, Representatives Pittenger, Hultgren, and Lieu.

OPENING STATEMENT OF HON. CHRISTOPHER SMITH, A U.S. REPRESENTATIVE FROM NEW JERSEY; CHAIRMAN, CONGRESSIONAL–EXECUTIVE COMMISSION ON CHINA

Chairman SMITH. The Commission will come to order. Good afternoon to everyone.

One year ago, U.S. Army Major Xiong Yan was barred from visiting his dying mother in China. Major Yan is blacklisted, denied access to China because he was a student leader of the democracy protests in 1989. Major Yan's mother passed away last year. Her son never had the chance to say goodbye.

The Communist leaders in Beijing use the blacklist along with intimidation, repression, and the lure of the Chinese market to stifle the discussion of the violence and oppression of the Tiananmen protests and their violent suppression that followed.

Academics such as Perry Link and Andrew Nathan are also blacklisted for writing about Tiananmen. U.S. corporations, eager to gain access to Chinese markets, also engaged in censorship about Tiananmen. Last year, the California-based LinkedIn began blocking Tiananmen-related articles posted inside China or by members hosted on its Chinese site.

Almost 10 years ago, I chaired a series of hearings on how Google and other Internet search engines had completely joined in with the repression and with the censorship. I will never forget we had Google CN, which was the Chinese version. We posted it and showed in the Foreign Affairs Committee Room what the average person would see in mainland China when they did a search on Tiananmen Square and even the massacre in 1989. Nothing but pretty pictures of folks, as compared to the hundreds of millions of hits you would get using Google in the United States or anywhere else.

(1)

The methods used by Beijing to enforce a code of silence have gone global. The heavy hand of the Chinese Government has expanded beyond its borders to intimidate and stifle critical discussion of the Chinese Government's human rights record and repressive policies.

Before I talk more broadly about our hearing today, let me first say a few words about the Tiananmen massacre.

The Commission has solemnly commemorated the Tiananmen massacre on and around June 4 each year. The Congress does this because of the lives that were lost and persons permanently injured in the massacre. We do so because of the profound impact the event had on U.S.-China relations and because so many former student leaders have made important contributions to the global understanding of China. We mark June 4th each year because the Chinese people are unable to mark this event themselves.

This year, the Congress is not in session on June 4th, but Senator Rubio and I will be sending a letter to President Xi Jinping asking him to allow uncensored, public discussion of the democracy protests of 1989—to end retaliation efforts against those who participated in the protests and to release all of those still detained for holding commemorations about the Tiananmen protests and their violent suppression.

We will urge President Xi to allow discussion of China's past history. We believe transparency is in the best interest of the U.S.-China relations and will improve global perceptions of China.

President Xi Jinping, however, seems to have a different conception of what is in China's interest. As is well-documented already in this Commission, his government is engaged in an extraordinary assault on civil society and advocates for human rights. China is not only interested in containing the spread of ''Western values and ideas'' within China, but is actively engaged in trying to roll back democracy and human rights norms globally.

In fact, it would be fitting to have an empty chair at the witness table today representing every dissident fearful of sharing their story, every writer whose work has been censored or edited by Chinese authorities without their knowledge, and every journalist whose critical reporting has been blocked or tempered—not just in China, but in the West.

China's recent efforts to blunt scrutiny of its rights record and criticism of government policies include pushing Thailand and Cambodia to forcibly repatriate Uyghur refugees and Chinese asylum seekers; disappearing and allegedly abducting five Hong Kong booksellers, including the father of one of our witnesses today; supporting clandestine efforts to discredit the Dalai Lama through a Communist Party-supported rival Buddhist sect; harassing and detaining the family members of foreign journalists and human rights advocates—two of our witnesses today will attest to such harassment; threatening the operations of non-governmental organizations engaged in work in China through the newly passed Overseas NGO Management Law and through other means.

Dr. Teng will talk about the cancellation of his book project by the American Bar Association [ABA]. We asked—Senator Rubio and I—the ABA to testify today, but the ABA President Paulette Brown and the ABA's CEO Jack Rives were not available to testify on this day. We will open the possibility to any day that they would like to come and speak to our Commission in an open hearing.

The ABA sent a letter to the Commission last month, however, responding to an inquiry by the Commission about the details surrounding their rescinding of the Teng book project. They want that letter to serve as their testimony. I would hope that they would go beyond it, and come here and face us and answer legitimate questions posed by Members of the Commission.

A copy of the Commission's letter to the ABA and the ABA response will be added to the record without objection.

The long reach of China extends beyond its borders to Thailand, South Korea, Malaysia, India, Kenya, at the United Nations, and in the United States.

These efforts present real strategic implications for the United States and the international community. The abductions of the booksellers challenge the ''one country, two systems'' model in Hong Kong. China's efforts to bend international human rights norms present a clear challenge to the United Nations and the Human Rights Council's efforts to hold China accountable. China's efforts to enforce a code of silence, globally, through its economic and diplomatic clout directly challenge the Obama Administration's ''Asia Pivot'' and U.S. human rights diplomacy.

The President and his Administration have only a few more chances to seriously raise human rights concerns with China: the Strategic and Economic Dialogue in two weeks and the G–20 meeting in September.

Congress and this Commission will press the Administration to do more to advance human rights in China. President Obama must ''shine a light'' on human rights problems in China because nothing good happens in the dark. And glib talk and pious platitudes simply do not cut it.

But we must also look ahead, use our Commission hearings, our Annual Report, and other publications to make a compelling case for the next Administration about the centrality of human rights to U.S. interests in Asia.

It is increasingly clear that there is a direct link between China's domestic human rights problems and the security and prosperity of the United States. The health of the U.S. economy and environment, the safety of our food and drug supplies, the security of our investments and personal information in cyberspace, and the stability of the Pacific region will depend on China's complying with international law, allowing the free flow of news and information, complying with its WTO obligations, and protecting the basic rights of Chinese citizens, including the fundamental freedoms of religion, expression, assembly, and association.

Losing sight of these facts leads to bad policy, bad diplomacy, and the needless juxtapositioning of values and interests. It also sends the wrong message to those in China standing courageously for greater freedoms, human rights, and the rule of law. The human rights lawyers, the free press advocates, and those fighting for labor rights, religious freedom, and democracy are the best hope for China's future. And, they are the best hope for a more stable and prosperous U.S.-China relationship.

I would like to now yield to our distinguished Cochair, Senator Marco Rubio.

[The letters appear in the appendix.]

[The prepared statement of Representative Smith appears in the appendix.]

STATEMENT OF HON. MARCO RUBIO, A U.S. SENATOR FROM FLORIDA; COCHAIRMAN, CONGRESSIONAL–EXECUTIVE COMMISSION ON CHINA

Senator RUBIO. Thank you very much, and thank all of you for being here today.

Next week marks the 27th anniversary of the student-led popular protests in Tiananmen Square. It was spurred by the death of a prominent reformer. Thousands gathered in April 1989 seeking greater political freedom

Their numbers swelled as the days passed, not only in Beijing but in cities and universities across the nation. Eventually, more than a million people, including journalists, workers, government employees, and police, joined their ranks—making it the largest political protest in the history of communist China.

And then late in the evening of June 3, the Army opened fire on peaceful protesters. The bloodshed continued until the next day. To this day, the precise number of resulting casualties is unknown and more than a quarter of a century later, there has been no progress toward a public accounting of the events of that fateful week.

Instead, 27 years later, the Chinese Government is increasingly brazen in its repression—no longer limiting its reach to China's territorial boundaries but instead seeking to stifle discussion of its deplorable human rights record, both at home and abroad. In that context, consider the following: Dissidents regularly report that their family members who remain in China are harassed, and detained, and even imprisoned in retaliation for their truth-telling about the regime's abuses. News reports abound of Uyghur Muslim and Chinese asylum-seekers being forcibly repatriated from neighboring Southeast Asian countries under pressure from the Chinese Government.

Journalists and academics alike are threatened with visa revocations, thereby allowing self-censorship to take root in what should be the very bastions of free expression and inquiry. Even educational institutions based here in the United States are not immune as more have welcomed the establishment of Confucius Institutes.

While seemingly benign at face value, the financial support that accompanies these centers for Chinese language and cultural education come with definite strings attached. Sensitive topics, including Taiwan and Tibet, are excluded from the curriculum, and invitations for the Dalai Lama to speak at prominent universities are mysteriously withdrawn.

In 2014, the American Association of University Professors issued a statement calling on colleagues across the United States and Canada to reconsider their partnerships with these centers, stating that, "The Confucius Institutes function as an arm of the Chinese state and are allowed to ignore academic freedom."

In April 2016, the Indian government blocked several rights advocates and activists from attending an Interfaith/Interethnic Conference in Dharamsala, India reportedly due to Chinese Government pressures to rescind their visas.

Last month, a news story broke alleging that the American Bar Association had canceled a proposed book project with prominent Chinese human rights lawyer Teng Biao, who we will hear from today. Multiple news sources reported that the project was canceled because of fears that the initiative would offend the Chinese Government. The ABA has denied these reports, claiming that the staff person in question who had interfaced with Teng Biao had been misinformed. Yet questions remain not only about the specifics of the book project but more broadly about the ability of groups like the ABA to continue working in China without compromising its principles.

And, of course, any discussion of the long arm of Beijing must include recent troubling developments in Hong Kong, specifically the disappearance and alleged abductions of five Hong Kong booksellers, which have rightly raised alarm bells among Hong Kong activists, human rights organizations, and foreign governments. The Commission will have the distinct privilege today to hear from Angela Gui, the daughter of missing bookseller Gui Minhai, a naturalized Swedish citizen who disappeared in October 2015 from Pattaya, Thailand.

In the recent State Department Hong Kong Policy Act report to Congress, the Department rightly noted that, ''These cases have raised serious concerns in Hong Kong and represent what appears to be the most significant breach of the 'one country, two systems' policy since 1997.''

In a sad testament to the timeliness and importance of today's hearing topic, some of the witnesses the Commission approached with an invitation to testify declined based on very legitimate fears about what would happen to members of their family who remain in China. This is an inexcusable reality.

For too long, China has gotten a free pass. The Obama Administration's final U.S.-China Strategic and Economic Dialogue is just days away in Beijing. Will these issues be prioritized? Will every participating U.S. government agency be charged with bringing human rights to the forefront with their Chinese counterparts? Will there be consequences for China's bold and aggressive disregard for human rights and extraterritorial reach?

In March, the United States spearheaded a collective statement at the U.N. Human Rights Council voicing serious concern about a number of issues to include the unexplained recent disappearances and apparent coerced returns of Chinese citizens and foreigners to China. The upcoming S&ED will be a litmus test for this Administration. The statement was commendable, but will words translate into action?

Thank you.

Chairman SMITH. Thank you, Chairman Rubio.

Commissioner Randy Hultgren?

[The prepared statement of Senator Rubio appears in the appendix.]

STATEMENT OF HON. RANDY HULTGREN, A U.S. REPRESENTATIVE FROM ILLINOIS

Representative HULTGREN. Well, thank you. I will be very brief. I want to get to our witnesses as quickly as possible.

I do want to thank Chairman Rubio. I appreciate your work on this, and Chairman Smith as well. This is so important, and I am grateful for this hearing today. I really want to echo what our Co-chairman has said, that this is our responsibility to continue to talk about the abuses that have happened, and continue to happen in China.

When things are swept under the rug, hidden, that we are lied to, frustration that we face when our own people here, Administration or others, might say, "Well, we do not want to rock the boat." Well, you know what? Lives are at stake and we need to do everything that we can to speak up for those who cannot speak up for themselves.

So that is why this hearing is so important, why we must never forget what happened 27 years ago on June 4, and continue to do everything we possibly can for every person and for every life to have the value that it deserves.

So thank you, witnesses, for being here. We want to work with you. We know your families, your own future is often in danger, and we want to work with you, fight for you, and fight for freedom for every single person.

So with that, Chairman Smith, Chairman Rubio, I yield back. Thank you.

Chairman SMITH. Thank you, Randy. I would like to now begin with our witnesses, first with Dr. Teng Biao, a well-known human rights lawyer; Visiting Fellow at the Harvard Kennedy School and the U.S.-Asia Institute, NYU Law School; and the Co-founder of the Open Constitution Initiative.

Dr. Teng holds a Ph.D. from Peking University Law School and has been a visiting scholar at Yale Law School. He is interested in the research on human rights, judicial systems, constitutionalism, and social movements.

As a human rights lawyer, Dr. Teng is a promoter of the Rights Defense Movement and co-initiator of the New Citizens' Movement in China. In 2003, he was one of the "Three Doctors of Law" who complained to the National People's Congress about unconstitutional detentions of internal migrants.

Since then, Dr. Teng has provided counsel in numerous other human rights cases, including those of Chen Guangcheng, and rights defender Hu Jia, and many other religious freedom and death penalty cases.

We will then hear from Angela Gui, who is a 22-year-old final-year undergraduate sociology student at the University of Warwick in the United Kingdom. As the daughter of disappeared Hong Kong bookseller, Gui Minhai, she has followed and worked actively on his case with governments, police, and various human rights groups since his disappearance in October of 2015.

She also did a brief internship with his and Lee Bo's company, Mighty Current Distributions, in the summer of 2014. Aside from her studies and work on her father's case, Ms. Gui is also editor and creative director of Warwick Sociology Journal, an academic journal showcasing undergraduate and graduate students' work from universities worldwide.

After graduation, Ms. Gui plans on continuing on to a master's degree in the history of medicine.

We will then hear from Ilshat Hassan, who is the President of the Uyghur American Association. Born in Ghulja, in Xinjiang, he taught at a college in Shihezi in Xinjiang for 15 years.

In November 2003, his teaching career abruptly ended due to his political activities. He fled to Malaysia, leaving behind parents, a wife, and a teenage son. Mr. Hassan came to the United States as a refugee in July 2006. He soon after joined the Uyghur American Association where he became a very active Uyghur human rights campaigner.

He writes in blogs, frequently in Chinese, and is well-known in the overseas Chinese democracy community.

Finally, we will hear, then, from Su Yutong who is a Chinese journalist and human rights defender. Because of her involvement in commemoration of the events linked to the Tiananmen massacre, she was invited for tea and for chats by the Chinese authorities and kept under surveillance, and periodically placed under house arrest.

In 2010, after she distributed Li Peng's diary, her home in China was raided, and documents were confiscated by the police. After leaving China in 2010, she started working in Bonn with Deutsche Welle, the German international broadcaster.

On July 4, 2014, however, a Beijing-based media consultant claimed in Deutsche Welle that some Western media were unfairly critical of the Chinese Government's crushing of the Tiananmen Square demonstrations. Ms. Su then became one of the most outstanding voices against this whitewashing of the 1989 events. In August of 2014, Deutsche Welle ended their employment relationship with her, sadly.

I would like to now go to Dr. Teng who is coming to us via Skype. [Pause.]

Dr. Teng, if you could begin your testimony. And if the camera man could move it a little to your right because you are way off on our left, your right.

STATEMENT OF TENG BIAO, CHINESE HUMAN RIGHTS LAWYER; VISITING FELLOW, HARVARD KENNEDY SCHOOL AND THE U.S.-ASIA INSTITUTE, NYU LAW SCHOOL; AND CO–FOUNDER, OPEN CONSTITUTION INITIATIVE

Mr. TENG. Can you hear me now?

Chairman SMITH. Better. A little bit more. We are seeing your chin and not your full face.

Mr. TENG. Can you hear me? Should I start?

Chairman SMITH. Yes, please start. But if you could move to your left if you would.

Mr. TENG. Okay. Thank you very much for your promoting human rights in China.

In 2014, the American Bar Association [ABA] invited me to write a book in which I would describe the decade I spent engaged in human rights work in China, my experience of disbarment, being kidnapped, being tortured, and my views on China's politics, judicial system, society, and future. But the formal offer of the ABA was soon rescinded. The Executive Director of ABA publishing wrote to me: "There is a concern that we run the risk of upsetting the Chinese Government by publishing your book. And because we have ABA commissions working in China, there is a fear that we would put their work at risk."

So this is a typical case of censorship, but I do not want to single out ABA. It is simply an example of the corrosive effect of the Communist party on the West. I had the experience of my scheduled speech being canceled by a university in the United States. The reason given to me was exactly the same as the ABA's.

The Confucius Institutes erode Western academic freedom. The "red capital" investment in Hong Kong and Taiwan media erode press freedom. Another example is cyberattacks on websites of foreign governments or institutions. [Internet connection lost.] [Pause.]

Chairman SMITH. While we wait to get Dr. Teng back, I would like to go to Angela Gui. When we get Dr. Teng back, we will put him on after your testimony.

STATEMENT OF ANGELA GUI, STUDENT AND DAUGHTER OF DISAPPEARED HONG KONG BOOKSELLER GUI MINHAI

Ms. GUI. Mr. Chairman Smith, Mr. Cochairman Rubio, Members of the CECC, thank you for inviting me to testify at this very important hearing, and thank you for the concern this Commission has shown for people like my father who are being persecuted by the Chinese Government in China, and now, increasingly, abroad.

As a university student, I never would have thought I would find myself testifying in front of the U.S. Congress, and certainly not under circumstances like these.

However, on October 13, 2015, I had my last Skype conversation with my father. Living in different places, we used to call each other on Skype regularly. I would tell him about how my studies were going, and he would tell me about work and how he was trying to get back into shape.

Our last Skype call was not very different. He had been renovating his kitchen in Hong Kong and sent me pictures of what it looked like, saying he would show me in person when it was finished.

We made plans to speak again in a few days, but then he stopped replying to my messages and emails, would not pick up when I called, and, about 3 weeks later, I received an email from his colleague, Lee Bo, saying my father had been missing for over 20 days and that he feared my father had been taken by Chinese agents for political reasons relating to his publishing business and bookstore.

I was later told that my father was last seen leaving his holiday apartment in Thailand with a man who had been loitering there, waiting for my father to return. I was also told that three of his colleagues at the bookstore had gone missing around the same time. We did not know that Lee Bo, himself, would be next.

Since then, the Chinese have detained my father without trial or charges. In November and in January, he sent me two messages on Skype, telling me to keep quiet. As his daughter, I could tell that he sent these under duress.

I did not hear or see anything of my father until a clearly staged and badly put together confession video of him was aired on Chinese state TV in January, three months after he was last seen. It failed to explain why they had held him without charge for three months and looked to me like they felt they needed to fabricate a justification in face of increasing media pressure.

Mr. Chairman, it has now been eight months since my father and his colleagues were taken into custody. I still have not been told where he is, how he is being treated, or what his legal status is, which is especially shocking in light of the fact that my father holds Swedish, and only Swedish, citizenship. In the so-called confession, my father says he travelled to China voluntarily, but if this is true, then we might ask why there is no record of him having left Thailand.

Only a state agency, acting coercively and against both International and China's own law, could achieve such a disappearance. By acting against my father and his colleagues, the Chinese are undermining their commitment to the ''One Country, Two Systems'' principle.

I want my testimony today to be a reminder to governments that despite the media having gone eerily quiet, my father, a Swedish citizen who was abducted by Chinese state agents from a third sovereign country, is still in unofficial and illegal detention somewhere in China, without access to consular visits or legal representation.

Despite having been told to stay quiet, I believe speaking up is the only option I have. Past cases clearly show that public criticism has had positive effects, and I am convinced my father would have done this for me, were I the one abducted and illegitimately detained without any indication of timeframe.

Therefore I am also here to ask for the Committee's help and support in working with the Swedish and other governments to demand my father's immediate release. Alternatively, if he is suspected of an actual crime, we ought to be given official details of his detention and proof that his case is handled according to established legal procedure.

I also want to ask the United States to take every opportunity to ask China for information on my father's status, as well as urge that he be freed immediately.

Finally, the United States, Sweden, and other countries concerned about these developments need to work to make sure that Chinese authorities are not allowed to carry out illegal operations on foreign soil.

Thank you.

Chairman SMITH. Thank you so very much for your testimony, Angela.

I would like to now—is Dr. Teng ready to come back? We will give it a shot, and if not, we will go to Mr. Hassan.

[The prepared statement of Ms. Gui appears in the appendix.]

STATEMENT OF ILSHAT HASSAN, PRESIDENT, UYGHUR AMERICAN ASSOCIATION

Mr. HASSAN. Thank you, Mr. Smith; thank you, Mr. Rubio; thanks everyone. I would like to first thank, also, the CECC for holding this important hearing today and for inviting me to participate. I am a victim of the Chinese Government's constant political persecution and a human rights activist living in the United States.

Personally, I hope the U.S. Government and U.S. Congress can understand the Chinese Government's long arm, which stretches beyond China's borders to overseas, to threaten and harass overseas human rights activists. I hope the U.S. Government and Congress will act to hold the Chinese Government accountable for its vicious actions.

My name is Ilshat Hassan Kokbore, also known as Ilshat Hassan. I was born in Ghulja, East Turkistan. The Chinese call it Xinjiang.

I have been politically active against communist Chinese rule in East Turkistan since studying at university in the 1980s. Constantly, I was under harassment, threats, and persecution from the regional government and secret agents, and police. I was, in university, beaten by police. And the police station also used an electric club to shock me. During work hours, I was frequently visited by the police, secret service, and I was also detained and beaten in the police station detention center, and my tooth was broken when they used the electric club to beat me.

Eventually, I was forced to leave East Turkistan in November 2003, leaving behind parents, sisters, a brother, wife, and an 11-year-old son. After I left China, when I was in Malaysia, my only brother—the youngest—was killed by a Chinese mob one year later, on November 27, 2004. I got the news a few months later in Malaysia, while waiting for the refugee resettlement through the UNHCR [UN High Commissioner for Refugees]. In July 2006, I came to the United States.

After coming to the United States, I joined the Uyghur community, joined the Uyghur American Association, and became active. I actively participated in all political campaigns organized by the Uyghur community, organizing demonstrations against the Chinese Government's occupation of East Turkistan, attending and holding conferences to expose the Chinese Government's cruel policy against the Uyghur people, and writing articles in Chinese to rebuke their claim over East Turkistan.

My political activities greatly agitated the Chinese Government. In the beginning, the Chinese Government held my family members hostage, denying my ex-wife and son passports; inhumanely causing the forced separation of my family. I was only able to meet with my son after 10 years of long-suffering separation. In 2014, I went to Malaysia and picked up my son—after 10 years.

After losing the hope of getting a passport for my ex-wife, and also to protect her from constant harassment from the Chinese Government, I had to make the painful decision to get a divorce. But that did not stop the Chinese Government from continuing to harass and threaten my ex-wife.

Recently, my son called me from Istanbul, Turkey and told me his mom—again—was visited by the Chinese police. My son sometimes asked me, "Can you be a little bit low profile, Dad, because mom is still there, under the Communist regime."

In order to pressure me to stop my political activities, on August 17, 2014, at midnight, Chinese regional authorities burst into my elder sister's house around 1:30 a.m. After searching her house and taking her son's computer, she was detained in an undisclosed place for around 8 to 10 months. I do not know when she was released. I know after eight months, she was not out.

Recently, my dad passed away. On the phone—I got my sister to pick up the phone, but she was not there to speak to me, just passed the phone to my mom. So I know she was released.

She was held without any charge, and she was a retired nurse, single mother with two kids. Her daughter graduated from university six years ago, and until now cannot get a job. Her son, in 2014, was accepted by a college.

When I called my home after my dad passed away, that is the only time since August 2014 I have been able to call my family; I had some—a little— conversation with my mom. She was telling me my sister's son could not go to university and is still staying at home with no job.

On the same day, August 17, 2014, RFA journalist Shohret Hoshur's two brothers were also detained, and were later sentenced. This was obvious retaliation against Mr. Hoshur, who revealed a great deal about Chinese police brutality against Uyghurs.

As we all know, prominent Uyghur leader, human rights champion, and World Uyghur Congress President Mrs. Rebiya Kadeer has constantly been accused by the Chinese Government of being an evil separatist, and her two sons were sentenced to jail as retaliation from the Chinese Government. The Chinese Government pressured one of Mrs. Kadeer's imprisoned sons to condemn his mother and to accuse Mrs. Kadeer of being an evil criminal. As normal, civilized human beings, we cannot imagine under what circumstances and under what kind of pressure a son was forced to condemn his dearest mother, accusing his own mother publicly of being a criminal.

Dolkun Isa, another prominent Uyghur human rights activist, and Chair of the World Uyghur Congress Executive Committee, was recently preparing to attend a meeting in Dharamsala, India. The Indian Government, after issuing a visa to Mr. Isa, and under the Chinese Government's pressure, cancelled the visa, denying Mr. Isa entry into India.

In late 2009, Mr. Isa, as a German citizen, was in immediate danger of being repatriated back to China when he tried to enter South Korea to attend a human rights conference. He was put in solitary confinement for more than three days in the airport before the United States and European Union intervened.

The Chinese Government has constantly tried to block all of Dolkun Isa's political activities by claiming he is a wanted terrorist according to an Interpol red notice, baselessly accusing him of supporting and funding terrorists.

Recently, another friend of mine, a Uyghur who is a Norwegian citizen, called me and told me that his family members living in

East Turkistan were being harassed by the Chinese Government. Some of his family members were brought to the police station and interrogated for several hours, and they were told to tell him to stop any activities supporting Uyghurs.

Of course, we all know about the Uyghur refugees who managed to get out of China. But unfortunately, they were sent back to China by some irresponsible countries when they were in the process of applying for UNHCR refugee status. Some of them were directly interrogated by Chinese police in other countries, in Malaysia, in Thailand, and in Kazakhstan, Uzbekistan, etc., and their family members were threatened. After they were repatriated, most of them disappeared, and some of them were given harsh sentences.

The story of Uyghurs facing the Chinese Government's constant persecution, harassment, and threats goes on and on. Even Uyghurs who live overseas cannot be spared from the inhuman political persecution of the Chinese Government. The Chinese Government's long arm keeps stretching longer and longer. It is obvious that if China is not pressured to stop this kind of harassment, no one will be safe, regardless of where we live.

Thank you all.

Chairman SMITH. Thank you very much, Mr. Hassan.

Ms. Su?

[The prepared statement of Mr. Hassan appears in the appendix.]

STATEMENT OF SU YUTONG, JOURNALIST, INTERNET ACTIVIST, AND FORMER NEWS BROADCASTER FOR THE CHINESE SERVICE OF DEUTSCHE WELLE

Ms. SU. My name is Su Yutong. I am a journalist and activist based in Germany. In June 2010, after I made public the personal diary of former Chinese Premier Li Peng, my house was ransacked by the police and I was forced to leave China.

In August that year, I became a journalist with the Chinese section of Deutsche Welle, where I wrote and published nearly 1,500 articles, most of which were about human rights and political affairs in China. The human rights lawyers and activists I reported on included Chen Guangcheng, Ilham Tohti, Gao Zhisheng, and Gao Yu. All of this work annoyed the Chinese Communist Party. Its state-owned newspaper Global Times attacked me in an article in August 2014, for ''constantly criticizing and vilifying China.''

Before I came to the United States to participate in this hearing, I was in contact with Chinese journalist Gao Yu and the family members of detained human rights lawyers. Gao, aged 72, had already been jailed twice. She was arrested and sentenced to prison in April 2014, for a third time, on charges evidently fabricated by the Chinese Communist Party.

The real reason for her imprisonment was retaliation for an article she published in her Deutsche Welle column, Beijing Observation, which criticized Xi Jinping. I was her executive director at the time. Last November, after Gao Yu was released on medical parole, the University of Bonn hospital was preparing to provide comprehensive treatment for her. And the German Ambassador to China issued her a visa to Germany. But the CCP authorities prevented Gao from leaving China for her medical treatment and ordered that she remain silent.

Since July 9, 2015, the Chinese Government has been conducting a sweeping crackdown on human rights lawyers and activists. The wives of several detained lawyers asked me to bring two videos to this hearing. To this day, these women have been unable to visit their husbands in custody. No one knows what abuses these jailed lawyers and activists have been suffering.

These women are appealing, again, to the media and the international community for assistance. I would like to request to show these two video clips at this hearing.

At this hearing today, there is not enough time to tell the stories of all the human rights activists in China. [Showing of a video clip.]

All three lawyers featured in this video clip, I know them well. I have met them when I was working in China. Later on, I interviewed them. I was in touch with them when I was working for Deutsche Welle in Germany.

Since Xi Jinping took power, China's human rights conditions have worsened constantly. The most courageous and outstanding people in China today are in prison or on the way to prison.

I am hoping such a human rights disaster in China will receive more international media coverage and more attention from the international community. But there is one dangerous trend—that is how the Chinese Communist Party has reached its arms of news control overseas, as part of its ''Great Overseas Propaganda Strategy.'' Such strategies include cross-border censorship and infiltration, attempting to muzzle international media in their coverage of China's worsening human rights conditions. As a journalist, I urge the Congress to pay more attention to this reality.

In 2011, Li Congjun, the head of Xinhua News Agency, described in an article in the Wall Street Journal the ''new global media order.'' Hundreds of Confucius Institutes proliferate around the world as an important part of China's overseas propaganda campaign. The Chinese Government has been pouring large sums of money in buying up overseas newspapers and radio networks.

Benjamin Ismail, Asia Director of Reporters Without Borders (RSF) says RSF found a number of digital radio stations in Paris that had been secretly run by proxy companies operated by the Chinese Government. In November 2015, Reuters also reported that WCRW, a radio station based in Washington, DC, has China International Radio, a Communist Party mouthpiece, as its hidden major shareholder.

According to an investigation by Reuters, there are already 33 radio stations around the world that are affiliated with China International Radio. Numerous media outlets with the Chinese Government as the controlling shareholder are scattered around the world. And they hire local workers. At the press conferences during the annual sessions of National People's Congress and the Chinese People's Political Consultative Conference in Beijing, CCP officials invited reporters from fake overseas media to ask pre-arranged, non-sensitive questions.

Buying off and cracking down. Those are the two tactics being adopted in Hong Kong—once a paradise for books banned in China. Hong Kong publisher Yao Wentian was sentenced to 10 years' im-

prisonment in China for publishing the book "Xi Jinping, The Godfather of China." French journalist Ursula Gauthier was expelled
by Beijing in late 2015 for her reporting and commentaries on
Xinjiang. In March of this year, relatives of New York-based activist Wen Yunchao—also known as Bei Feng—and German-based political commentator Chang Ping were detained and interrogated in
relation to an open letter calling on Xi Jinping to resign.

Under the CCP's media control, a number of overseas and online
Chinese language media outlets have been serving as platforms to
learn about a real China. When I was young, I secretly listened to
Voice of America, which was and is still banned in China. These
media outlets have now become targets of the Chinese Communist
Party's incessant efforts at control. Chinese embassies and consulates around the world have started to play the role of Ministry
of Propaganda.

In 2013, my former employer Deutsche Welle hired Peter
Limbourg as its new director. Soon after he assumed the post, Mr.
Limbourg paid a visit to the Chinese division of Deutsche Welle
and told the staff that he had met with Shi Mingde, China's Ambassador to Germany. Mr. Limbourg demanded that the Chinese
division not always criticize the Chinese authorities and should
"appropriately encourage" them instead.

In 2014, Mr. Limbourg hired Frank Sieren, a German businessman who is a long-term resident of Beijing, and who has businesses with Chinese Communist Party mouthpieces, such as the
Global Times. Mr. Sieren has had numerous business corporations
with other Chinese Communist Party outlets such as China Central TV.

In September 2014, German newspaper Süddeutsche Zeitung reported the minutes of an April meeting between Deutsche Welle
and China's Ambassador to Germany, which clearly revealed that
the Chinese Embassy demanded that Deutsche Welle change.

On June 4, 2014, Frank Sieren published an article in Deutsche
Welle, in German and Chinese languages, describing Tiananmen
Massacre as "a slip-up by the Chinese Communist Party." The
piece sparked a public outcry from a number of pro-democracy activists and massacre survivors, including Mr. Fang Zheng, who had
both legs crushed by a tank during the massacre.

I was a signatory to an open letter protesting this article. I spoke
up against the article on Twitter. Soon afterward, the deputy director and the director of Deutsche Welle Chinese division, both of
whom were highly critical of Mr. Sieren's article, were shifted to
other positions. Meanwhile, I was fired by Deutsche Welle.

In late August 2014, Mr. Limbourg traveled to Beijing to attend
a Chinese-German media symposium hosted by the Chinese Communist Party mouthpiece Global Times. At the same time, I published an open letter to him in the New York Times saying that
"the voice of China" is currently attempting to use economic seduction and coercion to expand its "great overseas propaganda" campaigns around the world.

My wishful thinking was that Mr. Limbourg, under the warm reception of Global Times, would not be drowned in Chinese wine
and succumb to becoming a tool in the Chinese Communist Party's
"overseas propaganda campaigns." But much to my regret, Mr.

Limbourg met with Wang Gengnian, the head of China Radio International, in Beijing on August 28, 2014. Mr. Limbourg said that Deutsche Welle's coverage would fit into the guidance and direction set by China. Soon afterward, he announced a cooperative framework between Deutsche Welle and China Central Television.

In early 2015, Germany's Bundestag took note of this cooperation program and conducted a hearing. Deutsche Welle announced that it would temporarily suspend its cooperation with CCTV.

Meanwhile, Frank Sieren continues to write a column for Deutsche Welle [DW]. In 2008, another scandal took place at Deutsche Welle, when a DW reporter named Zhang Danhong lied on a German TV program that the human rights conditions in China were excellent. She was moved to another division at Deutsche Welle after protests from a large number of members of the audience and pro-democracy activists. But in early 2015, Ms. Zhang was quietly returned to the Chinese department of DW and was given her own column.

Meanwhile, the former columnist for DW, journalist Gao Yu, who was detained in Beijing—her column was not revived even after her release. All of these changes are sending subtle signals.

The Chinese Communist Party has been continuously expanding its scope of censorship. On May 10, German legislator Michael Brand told the media that he was denied entry to China because of his criticism of China's Tibet policy. Mr. Brand, Chairman of the Committee on Human Rights and Humanitarian Aid of the German Bundestag, said the Chinese Embassy in Germany sent people to meet with him in person, demanding that he delete his articles on Tibet from his official website. They also demanded that Mr. Brand not attend a meeting with a Tibetan human rights organization.

Mr. Brand said, ''Such behaviors by the Chinese Communist Party are blatant and absurd, and it is unacceptable that the Chinese Communist Party exports its censorship to Germany.''

Mr. Brand's stance was very clear and of great importance. We hope politicians in countries around the world dare to say ''no'' to the Chinese Communist Party. In recent years, as China has achieved economic progress, numerous countries choose silence and compromise on China's human rights abuses in exchange for contracts with the Chinese Government. The most notable is the U.S. President, Barack Obama, who has been very weak and compromising when facing China's human rights issues.

The Chinese Government, nowadays, dares to reach its long arms to control the world. One factor is the brutal politics since Xi Jinping took power. The other reason is the appeasement from a number of countries.

As a media worker, I urge democratic countries to take notice of the Chinese Communist Party's propaganda campaigns overseas, and its infiltration and disturbance of the freedom of press. The United States and other countries should organize investigations into China's infiltration of press freedom and media outlets established by the Chinese Communist Party.

As a human rights activist, I am here to criticize and expose the increased crackdowns and persecution of human rights activists by the Chinese Communist government, especially under Xi Jinping's regime. I hereby request democratic governments not to neglect human rights conditions in China. Former U.S. President John F. Kennedy said in his speech at West Berlin's city hall in 1963, "Freedom is indivisible, and when one man is enslaved, all are not free."

Finally, please allow me to express my gratitude to CECC's continuous focus on China's human rights conditions and assistance to activists all along. My special thanks to Congressman Chris Smith and Senator Marco Rubio.

Chairman SMITH. Su Yutong, thank you very much for your testimony.

I think we are ready for Dr. Teng again. At least I have been told that. Yes.

Dr. Teng, if you could continue your testimony and if you could move to your left because we can only see half of you.

[The prepared statement of Ms. Su appears in the appendix.]

STATEMENT OF TENG BIAO (Continued)

Mr. TENG. Okay. Thank you. I am sorry for the disconnection. That is an example of CCP's long arm. I will continue my testimony.

Some Western journalists have been forced out of China or denied visas. Books and movies were partly changed or deleted when entering the Chinese market. Many Western scholars of China practice self-censorship—if their conclusions on a "sensitive" topic anger the regime, they will not get a visa, and their position and funding will be jeopardized.

Chinese and Tibetan activists living in California, Paris, or London were physically attacked when participating protests. More and more restrictions on the peaceful protests applied or organized by Chinese, Tibetan, and Uyghur activists when Chinese leaders visit Western countries. This of course has hurt the freedom and rule of law of the West. [Indiscernible.]

Chairman SMITH. Dr. Teng, if you could suspend for a moment. It is garbled. The connection is not good. Maybe we could try to fix that and come back to you one last time if we could. So we will try to fix that connection, but it is garbled.

Without objection, your full statement will be made a part of the record.

And I will mention some of it in my comments because it is so brilliantly written and it tells a story that needs to be told. So I want to thank you. If we could get this connection cleared up, we will do so.

Let me begin with some questions to our distinguished witnesses. Just to point out, Dr. Teng makes very serious points, which unfortunately, we could not hear from his own lips.

He talks about how his book—he was invited by the ABA to write a manuscript that was to be called Darkest Before the Dawn. In it, he would describe a decade that he spent engaged in human rights work in China and what those experiences illustrate about the country's politics, judicial system, and society.

Yet, then he was told by the American Bar Association—again, the very people who invited him to write this—and I will quote from the email. "I have some bad news," wrote an ABA employee,

''My publisher, after receiving some concerns from other staff members here about your proposed book, has asked me to rescind the offer that I made for Darkest Before Dawn on December 9. Apparently, there is concern that we run the risk of upsetting the Chinese Government by publishing your book.''—the employee wrote.

Let me just say, and all of you might want to comment on this—a tale of two stories—story number one, they got back later and said it was for economic reasons. To the best of my knowledge, the ABA is very well-endowed with finances. When they write books on human rights, it is not to turn a profit. It is to tell a story, and a story that must be told. Who better to tell it than Dr. Teng?

My sense, as a Member of Congress for 36 years, and working on Chinese human rights for 36 years, of the human rights abuses around the world, is that it appears the ABA capitulated, caved. We have invited them to be here. We will invite them again because I would like to ask very specific questions.

I do believe it is enabling of a dictatorship when a group with such a reputation as the ABA turns down a book like this out of fear of retaliation. It becomes the modus operandi of so many like Deutsche Welle and others who cave into the pressure.

As Dr. Teng points out—any of you want to respond to this—he says he does not want to single out the ABA, although that is with whom he has had the problem. But says it is the latest example of the corrosive influence of the Chinese Communist Party on the west. He talks about Yahoo. We have had hearings in my Subcommittee on Human Rights in this Commission that I have chaired about how Yahoo has turned over the names of dissidents when asked and Shi Tao got 10 years simply for telling people about the upcoming Tiananmen Square efforts by the government to suppress.

He points out in his testimony that Facebook is flirting with the Chinese market. Twitter has just hired a former Chinese military and security apparatchik to head their operations in China—that is not an ominous sign.

Su Yutong, you talked about posting your comments on Twitter. Well, I would think Twitter is certainly that which would be found in China would become increasingly off limits to any kind of dissident.

Then he makes a very good point about the ABA might imagine, for instance, that the All China Lawyer's Association is their professional counterpart. It has been my experience that the Chinese Government and other dictatorships always want to have this twinning with what appears to be like-minded organizations. The Chinese National Peoples' Congress with the U.S. Congress, sending over delegations as if they are elected by the population as opposed to be the party apparatchik.

Finally, he does point out—and you might want to respond to this as well—that the rule of law human rights dialogues, meanwhile, have mostly become a means for the party to deflect substantive demands to change its human rights practices. Dialogues end with vague remarks about the importance of dialogue and the understanding in the ongoing nature of the reform process without producing results.

The United States, another country, but a similar dictatorship in Vietnam, has lifted the arms embargo on lethal weapons—as we all know—without any conditionality on human rights, without any, zero. We have appealed to him—me and others, many others—asking—including the New York Times in an editorial—not to do this. So we get a reprise of the same flawed policy of the United States.

I would note, Su Yutong, you point out the most notable is the U.S. President Obama who has been very weak in compromising when facing Chinese human rights issues. That is an understatement. But I appreciate the candor. Forget political correctness. Real wonderful people are tortured—and we just had a hearing on torture in this Commission—with impunity, and there is barely a voice of dissent, and certainly no linkage to trade or arms control deals as we are seeing in Vietnam when this egregious behavior manifests itself as it does.

So if any of you would like to touch on anything that I have said here, please do.

To Angela Gui, Hong Kong, unlike mainland China, has historically enjoyed greater press freedom—we all know that—and freedom of expression. Do you know why the Chinese authorities targeted your father and his company? Is it part of a growing crackdown? Secondly, has the U.S. Government and other like-minded governments—what have they done to help your father? For example, has the Swedish government responded to your requests regarding your father's case?

[The prepared statement of Mr. Teng appears in the appendix.]

Ms. GUI. Well, I would like to say that I am very grateful for all the help and support I have had from the Swedish government. However, I do believe that its resources have not been exhausted completely yet.

I would like to ask the United States and other governments to keep asking questions and to keep raising it with China, both privately and publicly.

As for Hong Kong, it has not been clear what my dad, officially, is in Chinese custody for. I have not had any written confirmation of his being in detention. I have not had a formal detention notice. So I do not know what the official reason is. However, it seems to me that it is quite clear that he is there because of his work.

I suppose that is why all of his coworkers are there as well, or have been there. They have nominally been released. Lee Bo, for example, has been made to return more than once.

Chairman SMITH. Let me ask you, Mr. Hassan, the Chinese Government notoriously not only puts pressure, but also incarcerates family members, particularly of dissidents. Rebiya Kadeer has testified here before, as you know.

We know that India's recent revocation of the World Uyghur Congress Executive Committee Chairman Dolkun Isa's visa, reportedly, was due to Chinese pressure. If you could speak to the issue of this harassment, incarceration, and torture of family members, which has to be the cruelest cut of all, to take it out on one's loved ones, which is what is happening to the Uyghurs and others, but also the influence on other governments like India and there are other governments as well.

Mr. HASSAN. Thank you, sir. Definitely—we were facing—the Chinese Government prosecution is unprecedented. It is to understand almost like a black hole. We do not know what is going on over there. It is in the news, killing, shooting, and arresting.

Personally, my sister's detention, it was very sudden because of my writing in the Chinese websites about government—what they are doing in east Turkistan, cracking down. We were arrested—given the reason at the time when I had conversation with my second sister, they said only the regional authority asked to detain my sister. And they could only send money and clothes. No visits allowed.

That same day, actually, it was not only my sister. Also the Radio Free Asia journalist Shohret Hoshur's brother—also it was the same day, he got arrested in—my sister was in—another city, another 500 kilometers away city, and they would get arrested.

So in the jail they are facing solitary confinement. What else happened, because of the cut off of communication, after that I was only able to call my father's cell phone before he passed away last month. My father only picked up the phone to say, son, we are okay. Keep safe. Then he would drop the phone.

So that is the reality. I do not know what happened to my sister over there, or how long she was detained. It was at least for eight months, I am sure, because that time I got another message from my son saying she is not released yet.

Regarding the Dolkun Isa—overseas activity—Dolkun Isa was frequently stopped by some countries that were under the Chinese pressure. One was South Korea in late 2009. He was involved in an international human rights conference, to attend Seoul. When he was entering South Korea, in the airport, he was detained. They put him in airport confinement, solitary confinement, and for more than three days he lost contact. His was only able to send a few messages to outside.

Then because of the United States' intervention and the German European Union, finally he was put back on the German airplane.

Recently, last month—the end of last month—Dr. Yang Jianli, he organized a religious ethnic groups conference in Dharamsala. The Uyghur Congress initially gave the names of eight delegates. Finally, I am the only to make that trip. Others—Dolkun Isa's visa became a big point in the newspaper. He was issued a visa, and then it was cancelled.

Over there, we met with some dignitaries. We asked them—they were saying because Dolkun Isa was in the Red Notice of Interpol. But some journalists did a search of Interpol's wanted list. Dolkun Isa's name was not there. He was only on the Chinese list, but still Chinese can have an impact on India's decisions and South Korea's decisions. Of course, other human rights activists are facing the same issue.

A few years back, also, the Uyghur leadership tried to visit India and some other countries. Taiwan also denied the visas.

Thank you.

Chairman SMITH. Thank you. I have some additional questions, but I would like to yield to Ted Lieu who has joined us.

Commissioner?

Representative LIEU. Thank you, Mr. Chairman.

Angela, thank you for being here. I have a few questions for you. I just want to make sure I understand this correctly.

Your father is a Swedish citizen?

Ms. GUI. Yes.

Representative LIEU. And only a Swedish citizen?

Ms. GUI. Yes.

Representative LIEU. Has Sweden taken action on this case?

Ms. GUI. They have, yes.

Representative LIEU. What have they done or requested?

Ms. GUI. They were allowed to meet him in February. They were not given any information until this video clip aired on Chinese TV. Before that, they were sending inquiries to the Chinese authorities asking if they knew anything, but I have been told that they were just told that they did not know anything. And they were asking Sweden why they were asking them since he disappeared in Thailand.

However, when this clip became public, it was quite clear where he was. So then after that, Sweden started sending inquiries to be able to speak with him or to meet with him. That was not granted until late February.

When they finally got to meet him, he told them that he did not want any help, and that he considered himself to be Chinese. And then he got up to leave is what I have been told.

In my understanding, they keep asking privately for more information on his charges, if there are any charges. They keep asking for further counselor access, which they have not been granted. They have not been given any proper answers to any of their questions.

Representative LIEU. Has the U.S. State Department done anything in this case?

Ms. GUI. Well, I read this report that was issued quite recently. I was quite happy with that. I would like to thank the U.S. State Department for doing that.

Representative LIEU. Is your father currently detained, or is he free to travel within a certain area, or what is your understanding of where he is?

Ms. GUI. That is very unclear. I actually do not know. I have not been told directly where he is even. I do not know where in China he is.

As I said earlier, there has not been any official detention notice. So officially, it would seem that he is just there.

I have had phone calls from him in which he has told me that I am not allowed to visit. But that he is going to be able to call me regularly which has not really happened.

That is, unfortunately, all I know.

Representative LIEU. When was the last phone call you had with your dad?

Ms. GUI. That was a bit over a month ago.

Representative LIEU. And China has not said anything about any sorts of charges?

Ms. GUI. No.

Representative LIEU. And then the alleged videotaped statements he made, what was the nature of those statements? What did they have him say?

Ms. GUI. Well, he said that he had returned to China on his own, and that he did not wish to have any help from the Swedish government or any institutions because he considered himself Chinese, even though he has Swedish citizenship. He also said that he returned because he felt remorse over a supposed drunk driving accident in which he is supposed to have killed a person. That is supposed to have been 12 or 13 years ago, I believe.

This is not anything that I have ever heard of. So I seriously doubt that it is something that even happened, and if it did happen, I am wondering why there has not been any order for his arrest.

I have spoken to the Swedish police, and I have been told that there has not been any reports to Interpol from China for my father's arrest. So it just seems very unlikely to me that—even if it would have happened, this accident—that this would have anything to do with it.

Representative LIEU. Do you believe he was making these statements freely or voluntarily?

Ms. GUI. Absolutely not.

Representative LIEU. At the time that he was abducted, was he remodeling? I read in your statement he is remodeling his kitchen in Hong Kong?

Ms. GUI. Yes.

Representative LIEU. So if you were to believe what China is saying, it would be in the middle of his remodel he just decided to up and leave and go to China, and stay there; right?

Ms. GUI. Yes. Without telling me beforehand, and we had even planned to speak in a few days after our last call, our last Skype call, which I mentioned in my statement. As his daughter, I was quite close to him. I am certain that he would have told me.

Representative LIEU. Right.

Ms. GUI. If he were to suddenly decide to go to China.

Representative LIEU. Right. Thank you for your testimony.

Ms. GUI. Thank you.

Representative LIEU. I yield back.

Chairman SMITH. Thank you very much, Commissioner.

I would like to ask Su Yutong, if you would. In your testimony, you spoke about how Mr. Limbourg said that Deutsche Welle's coverage would fit into the guidance and direction set by China. He announced the cooperative framework between Deutsche Welle and China Central Television, CCTV, in early 2015. But then the Bundestag took note of the cooperation and conducted a hearing, and that they temporarily suspended that cooperation.

One, is that still suspended, or are they cooperating now? Secondly, your termination was based on your criticism of China. What did the TV network tell you? For most news networks pursuing the truth unfettered and without fear is what they aspire to. Some do not live up to it, but when DW and others are compromised in this way, it certainly puts a—their reputation suffers as an objective news source.

I am wondering—in Germany, for example, or anywhere else, has DW's objectivity suffered as a result of your aspiring for speaking the truth about Chinese repression?

Ms. Su. Here I would like to ask all of you to continue your support to Deutsche Welle.

I just do not agree with Mr. Peter Limbourg's—what he said about when he paid a visit to the Chinese Division, not to criticize the Chinese Government too much. I think as a journalist, we should not be told what not to criticize and what to criticize.

When Peter Limbourg told us not to criticize the Chinese Government too much, I opposed it, and he clearly expressed that my opinion—such an opinion was not welcome.

When I was fired by DW, the reason they told me for sacking me was that I disclosed internal meetings, the information of internal meetings at DW on Twitter. But to me, this is a public affair. I have my responsibility to disclose it. This is not internal.

So the reason, they told me when they sacked me, was that I disclosed internal information of my employment, of my work. But to me, for DW, hiring somebody to write articles to whitewash the Tiananmen massacre, I think this is my responsibility to criticize them.

I actually to the matter to the court, and the court has made a verdict which I think is quite fair, but because of the legal issues, I cannot disclose any more information. But the judge did say she could see the political background in this case.

So during the hearing of German Bundestag there was extensive media coverage of the hearing. I did disclose that DW did sign with CCTV a framework of cooperation that they agreed to adopt the directives from China.

I did write numerous letters to German Bundestag, and I had meetings with the media committee of the Bundestag, and I did ask them not to talk too much about my personal case, but I did ask them to pay more attention to DW. That is why the German Bundestag held that hearing on Deutsche Welle signing the framework of cooperation with China Central TV, CCTV. After the suspension, I do not know how they will progress.

As for other media workers who became victims of this kind of censorship—for example, my former colleagues, the deputy director and the director of the Chinese Division of Deutsche Welle, they were moved to other positions after my case. The worst effect of my case is that many of my former colleagues at Deutsche Welle decided not to touch the so-called "sensitive topics." The key issue here is that the employees of Deutsche Welle, especially the Chinese Division, they chose to avoid certain sensitive topics, topics such as Tibetan—and Malaysians, and Xinjiang. So in choosing their coverage, Tibet and Xinjiang, they were very choosey in determining what to cover.

The biggest significance of my fight in this case is that it pushed the German Bundestag to conduct the hearing. As a result, it did pressure DW not to avoid human rights coverage too much.

But still, I am very unsatisfied with Deutsche Welle. For example, the columnist who wrote an article whitewashing the Tiananmen massacre, Frank Sieren, he continues to write his column. And in his column, he included his hidden praises of the Chinese Government. Another columnist I mentioned before, Zhang Danhong, continues to write her column as well.

My case is not an isolated case. After I was sacked, reporters from French Radio International contacted me and told me that they were censored by the Chinese Embassy. The Chinese Embassy in France pressured French Radio International.

I have been in touch with journalist from public broadcasters. I am still worried about such censorship, but I have been in touch with reporters from Voice of American, and I am happy to hear that they still take up the responsibility and uphold their ethical standards.

But as I said, the Chinese Embassies around the world have been increasingly taking up a role as the ''Ministry of Propaganda.''

Chairman SMITH. Thank you.

Mr. Lieu, anything further?

Representative LIEU. I would ask one more question to Angela. The Chinese Foreign Minister, I think, had made the remark that your father was, ''first and foremost a Chinese citizen.'' Were you aware of that remark?

Ms. GUI. Yes.

Representative LIEU. Had your father given up Swedish citizen?

Ms. GUI. No. He has not. I have been told that Chinese authorities have told Swedish authorities that he wished to do so. There have not been any papers filed to my knowledge.

Representative LIEU. Okay.

Ms. GUI. And this was after his disappearance.

Representative LIEU. Thank you. Just for the record, I find that statement from the Foreign Minister bizarre.

Ms. GUI. So do I.

Representative LIEU. So I yield back.

Chairman SMITH. Let me just conclude here. First of all, I want to note that Chen Guangcheng and his wife, Weijing are here, two wonderful human rights activists who have paid a dear price for their work, having suffered in prison for four years, and then even a similar amount of years—over three—under house arrest. Welcome to this hearing.

Dr. Yang Jianli is also here, President of Initiatives for China, who testified at our most recent hearing on torture. He is here somewhere. He may be in the back.

And there are others, very notable and brave individuals. Thank them for their work.

Let me just conclude—to Su Yutong and to all of you, I do believe that every time, every time the Chinese Government coerces a news organization, a policymaker, a government, and that entity yields, not only do they get away with impunity and in some cases murder, literally, but certainly human rights abuse of a very high degree. It only emboldens the Chinese Government to do more of it because it does yield results. I would hope that all news organizations—thank you for point out the VOA is very clear and does not stray and is not influenced. There are others like them.

But it is very disconcerting how quickly businesses, some corporations, particularly some like Google for so long, are willing to just sacrifice freedom and their commitment to human rights and democracy in order to get a piece of the rock to get some money. On the case of the corporations to have access—you mentioned— we were talking earlier about the fact that—I mentioned it, but Dr.

Teng, especially said that we could not hear his whole testimony—but the whole idea of censoring like that, and having the ABA—which again, I will ask again if they would like to come. We will offer the opportunity for the American Bar Association to testify as to why they revoked their offer to print a book that just needs to be published.

It reminds me of Stanford years ago, when the man that broke the story of coercive population control lost his doctorate—this was in the early 1980s—because it was an unpleasant truth and the Chinese Government pushed back on that University. It was so bad that a number of editorials were written, one by the Wall Street Journal. The title was Stanford Morality. It talked about how access to China trumped telling the truth about a hideous attack on women and women's rights and children through their coercive population control policy.

Unfortunately—and that is why we are having this hearing—this is part of a pattern. We held hearings recently, and we are going to do more. We are awaiting a GAO report on Confucius Institutes and the muzzling of American universities that have Confucius Institutes operating on their campuses to be a little more lax in their concerns about human rights.

Recently, I gave a keynote speech at NYU Shanghai, pointing out concerns about human rights, because it concerns—regarding that university. So it is an ongoing probe that this Commission is doing.

We should just speak truth to power, and let the chips fall where they may. And frankly, we would be amazed—I believe—on how it will at least on the edges, and then eventually at its core, transfer these societies that have embraced dictatorship. I am talking about at the point of a gun.

I thank our witnesses. You helped this Commission. I think we are going to have to wait, frankly, until the next Administration to see any meaningful action. Hopefully whoever wins will take Chinese human rights abuse seriously and not mishandle it the way it has been. I say that not as a partisan, but as someone who cares—like you—deeply about these issues. It is all about the vic- tim. It is all about the person who is suffering in the Laogai or some other place of detention.

Without objection, I would just like to ensure for the record, the transcript of the video of the wives that spoke earlier—words from wives of human rights lawyers in China will be made a part of the record.

And Wen Yunchao—his statement will also be made a part of the record.

Thank you so much to our witnesses for your bravery and for speaking truth to power. The hearing is adjourned.

[A transcript of the video clip appears in the appendix.]

[The prepared statement of Mr. Wen Yunchao appears in the appendix.]

[Whereupon the hearing was concluded at 1:55 p.m.]

APPENDIX

Prepared Statements

Prepared Statement of Teng Biao

May 24, 2016

The Cost of Self-Censorship in Dealing With China

In December 2014 I was invited by the American Bar Association (ABA) to write a manuscript for a book to be titled ''Darkness Before Dawn.'' In it, I would describe the decade I spent engaged in human rights work in China, and what those experiences illustrate about the country's politics, judicial system, society, and future.

But the formal offer with the ABA was soon rescinded. The reason, I was told by the executive director of ABA publishing, was because they were afraid to anger the Chinese government.

When ''Chinese politics'' is mentioned, most think of the factional struggles forever roiling Zhongnanhai, the headquarters of the Communist Party. But this is only part of the picture. The stories I've long sought to tell are otherwise: about the activists given heavy prison sentences for forming opposition political parties; about the human rights lawyers who've represented persecuted Christians, Falun Gong practitioners, Tibetans, and Uyghurs; about the rights defenders whose dogged activism helped to abolish the labor camp system. And then there are those who've worked against the one child birth control policy, forced demolitions, judicial misconduct, and environmental pollution, as well as the non-governmental organizations (NGOs) who have promoted democratic ideals, defended free speech, and pushed for greater gender equality.

I'm one of their number: for my activism I've been banned from teaching, been forced out of a job, had my passport confiscated, been disbarred from practicing law, and have even been jailed and tortured. All of us engaged in this work have paid an enormous price—but we've made progress. No understanding of contemporary China is complete without a thorough grasp of this community of Chinese activists. They're the country's hope for the future.

These were the ideas animating the manuscript proposal that was at first enthusiastically received by the ABA. It promised to be ''an important and groundbreaking book,'' my correspondent said. But the formal publishing contract we signed was soon reneged upon, with this explanation: ''There is concern that we run the risk of upsetting the Chinese government by publishing your book, and because we have ABA commissions working in China there is fear that we would put them and their work at risk.''

I don't want to single out the ABA. This is simply the latest example of the corrosive influence of the Chinese Communist Party on the West. I had the experience that my schedule speech was cancelled for the last minute by an American university, the reason given to me was exactly the same one as ABA. It's a crowded field: There are the Confucius Institutes and the Federations of Chinese Scholars and Students, both under the control of the Chinese government as they erode academic freedom on campuses in the United States. There's Yahoo, who provided China's public security forces with the personal information of Chinese political dissidents so authorities could arrest and jail them. Facebook is flirting with the China market. And Twitter just hired a former Chinese military and security apparatchik to head their operations in China. ''Red capital'' has flooded the media markets in Hong Kong and Taiwan, and some Western journalists have been forced out of China or denied visas. Books have had key passages deemed sensitive deleted. And many Western scholars of China practice self-censorship—for perfectly understandable reasons: if their conclusions on a ''sensitive'' political topic anger the regime, they won't get a visa, and their prestige, position, and funding will be jeopardized. Chinese and Tibetan activists living in San Francisco, London, Switzerland were attacked when participating in protests. Chinese activists, dissidents, publishers were kidnapped in Thailand or Burma and sent back to China, Some of them hold Swedish or UK passport.

The ABA is just one of the many major Western institutions attempting to promote change in China—on the Communist Party's terms. Alongside the ABA's Rule of Law Initiative, there's the U.S.-China Human Rights Dialogue, the EU–China Human Rights Dialogue, training programs for Chinese judges, prosecutors, and police, and exchange programs with universities and the official lawyers' associations. These organizations want their programs to be effective—and so they carefully avoid a great many issues that might endanger their success. The list is long: the persecution of Falun Gong, the Tiananmen Square massacre in 1989, the Party's policies in Tibet and Xinjiang, dissidents, "radical" human rights lawyers, and street activists. There is a constant guessing game about which way the political winds in Beijing are blowing. And so without realizing it, Western institutions end up helping the Chinese government to silence and marginalize the individuals and groups it finds the most troublesome. Self-censorship has become instinctive, and now characterizes the very basis of their interactions with the regime.

For the quiet sense of guilt that self-censorship engenders, there is a tempting comfort in the idea that: "Well, in the end we're still creating more space for the rule of law and human rights."

But the reality of foreign assistance has resulted in an unintended consequence. Nearly all the major program funding has ended up in the pockets of government departments, Government-Organized Nongovernmental Organizations (GONGOs), and scholars with state ties. Resources meant to support the rule of law and human rights have made their way into the hands of those whose job it is trample upon human rights: courts, Procuratorates, public security departments, the official lawyers association, and Party-affiliated mass organizations like the All-China Women's Federation.

Americans here are guilty of the classic error of mirror-imaging: projecting onto China what is familiar to them. The ABA might imagine, for instance, that the All China Lawyers Association (ACLA) is their professional counterpart. This would be a deep misunderstanding. My book discusses the extensive efforts by rights defense lawyers in Beijing to lobby for free elections for key positions in the ACLA, and how the attempts were shut down and those engaged in them punished. ACLA, and all Bar Associations in China, are simply part of the government's apparatus of control: it has disbarred numerous rights lawyers on the orders of the Party, and has been a proactive accomplice in drafting policies that prevent lawyers from taking on political cases. Helping these GONGOs is worse than doing nothing.

The same can be said for the training programs directed at police, judges, and prosecutors: Western organizations are inclined to think that miscarriages of justice must simply be a matter of insufficient professional training. Wrong again. The primary reason for abuses of justice in China is because the judicial system is an instrument of Party control, where political cadres directly and arbitrarily interfere in legal cases.

Foreign organizations are thus limited to working in the apolitical safe zones the regime tacitly permits. These include, for instance, environmental protection, better treatment for handicapped people, women's rights, HIV/AIDS, and education. Even in these sectors though, they're still treated as "hostile foreign forces." In the past few years, in particular, the regime's realm of permissiveness has rapidly constricted. And so we see that attempts to please the Communist Party with mild-mannered human rights promotion haven't brought about any concessions on the part of the authorities. The soon-to-be-passed Foreign NGO Management Law will further narrow the space in which these organizations can operate.

Rule of law and human rights dialogues, meanwhile, have mostly become a means for the Party to deflect substantive demands to change its human rights practices. Dialogues end with vague remarks about the importance of dialogue and understanding and the ongoing nature of the reform process. Yet rights defenders and journalists are arrested in still greater numbers. Torture, forced disappearances, detention in black jails, and religious persecution haven't decreased. When the Chinese activist Cao Shunli attempted to participate in the UN Human Rights Council's Universal Periodic Review, she was tortured to death. Other recent prominent cases include that of Tenzin Delek Rinpoche, a Tibetan monk, who died in jail in July 2015, and Ilham Tohti, a moderate Uyghur scholar, who was sentenced to life imprisonment last year. Both were peaceful activists. And then there is Nobel Peace Prize laureate Liu Xiaobo, who is still serving his 11 year sentence in prison.

Because the Party has already fixed the realm of the permissible, foreign organizations feel that they're limited to working only with official agencies and scholars. But those who need help the most, who deserve it the most, and who've taken the greatest risks for China's future, are excluded before a conversation can even begin.

If refusing to publish my book was the price to pay for genuinely effective work by ABA to promote the rule of law in China, then I would happily tear the contract up myself. But the opposite is true.

The permissive attitude and mild policies on China by international NGOs is of a piece with the West's general appeasement of China's dictatorship. It's an approach based on short-sighted interests, and it undermines the sanctity of universal values. Not only do these policies fail to promote human rights and the rule of law in China, but the relentless self-censorship has come to erode the moral prestige and values that are at the foundation of free societies. It's high time for a new approach.

PREPARED STATEMENT OF ANGELA GUI

MAY 24, 2016

Mr. Chairman Smith, Co-chairman Rubio,

Thank you for inviting me to testify at this important hearing, and thank you for the concern this Commission has shown for people like my father who are being persecuted by the Chinese government in China, and now, increasingly, abroad.

As a university student, I never would've thought I'd find myself testifying in front of the US congress, and certainly not circumstances like these.

On October 13th last year, I had my last Skype conversation with my father. Living in different places, we used to call each other on Skype regularly—I would tell him about how my studies were going, and he would tell me about work and how he was trying to get back into shape. Our last Skype call wasn't very different— he had been renovating his kitchen in Hong Kong and sent me pictures of what it looked like, saying he would show me in person when it was finished.

We made plans to speak again in a few days, but then he stopped replying to my messages and emails, wouldn't pick up when I called, and about three weeks later I received an email from his colleague Lee Bo saying that my father had been missing for over twenty days and that he feared my father had been taken by Chinese agents for political reasons relating to his publishing business and bookstore.

I was later told that my father was last seen leaving his holiday apartment in Thailand with a man who had been loitering there, waiting for my father to return. I was also told that three of his colleagues at the bookstore had gone missing around the same time. We didn't know that Lee Bo himself would be next.

Since then, the Chinese have detained my father without trial or charges. In November and in January, he sent me two messages on Skype telling me to keep quiet. As his daughter, I could tell he sent these under duress. I didn't hear or see anything of my father until a clearly staged and badly put together confession video of him was aired on Chinese state TV in January, three months after he was last seen. It failed to explain why they had held him without charge for three months and looked to me like they felt they needed to fabricate a justification in face of increasing media pressure.

Mr. Chairman, it has now been eight months since my father and his colleagues were taken into custody. I still haven't been told where he is, how he is being treated, or what his legal status is—which is especially shocking in light of the fact that my father holds Swedish, and only Swedish, citizenship. In the so-called confession my father says he travelled to China voluntarily—but if this is true, then why is there no record of him having left Thailand? Only a state agency, acting coercively and against both International and China's own law could achieve such a disappearance. By acting against my father and his colleagues, the Chinese are undermining their commitment to the "One Country, Two Systems" principle.

I want my testimony today to be a reminder to governments that despite the media having gone eerily quiet, my father, a Swedish citizen who was abducted by Chinese state agents from a third sovereign country, is still in unofficial and illegal detention somewhere in China, without access to consular visits or legal representation.

Despite having been told to stay quiet, I believe speaking up is the only option I have. Past cases show that public criticism has had positive effects, and I'm convinced my father would have done this for me, were I the one abducted and illegitimately detained without any indication of timeframe. Therefore I'm also here to ask for the committee's help and support in working with the Swedish and other governments to demand my father's immediate release. Alternatively—if he is suspected of an actual crime—we should be given official details of his detention and proof that his case is handled according to established legal procedure. I also want to ask the United States to take every opportunity to ask China for information on my father's status, and urge that he be freed immediately. Finally, the US, Sweden, and other countries concerned about these developments need to work to make sure that Chinese authorities are not allowed to carry out illegal operations on foreign soil.

Thank you.

PREPARED STATEMENT OF ILSHAT HASSAN KOKBORE

MAY 24, 2016

Good afternoon.

I would like to first thank the CECC for holding this important hearing today, and for inviting me to participate. I am a victim of the Chinese government's constant political persecution, and a human rights activist living in the United States.

Personally, I hope the U.S. government and U.S. Congress can understand the Chinese government's long arm, which stretches beyond China's borders to overseas, to threaten and harass overseas human rights activists. I hope the U.S. government and Congress will act to hold the Chinese government accountable for its vicious actions.

This is my personal story.

My name is Ilshat Hassan Kokbore, also known as Ilshat Hassan. I was born in Ghulja, East Turkistan.

I have been politically active against communist Chinese rule in East Turkistan since studying at university in the 1980s. Constantly under harassment, threats, and persecution from the regional government's secret service agency, I was forced to leave East Turkistan in November 2003, leaving behind my parents, sisters and brothers, wife, and child. After three years of waiting in Kuala Lumpur, Malaysia for resettlement as a refugee, in July 2006, I came to the United States.

After coming to the United States, I joined the Uyghur American Association (UAA) and became a very active member of UAA. I actively participated, organizing demonstrations against the Chinese government's occupation of East Turkistan, attending and holding conferences to expose the Chinese government's cruel policy against the Uyghur people, and writing articles in Chinese to rebuke their claim over East Turkistan.

My political activities greatly agitated the Chinese government. In the beginning, the Chinese government held my family members hostage, denying my wife and son passports; inhumanely causing the forced separation of my family. I was only able to meet with my son after 10 years of long-suffering separation.

After losing the hope of getting a passport for my wife, and also of protecting her from constant harassment from the Chinese government and secret agents, I had to make the painful decision to get a divorce. But that didn't stop the Chinese government from continuing to harass and threaten my ex-wife, and she was continually under surveillance and threats.

In order to pressure me to stop my political activities, on August 17, 2014, at midnight, Chinese authorities burst into my elder sister's house around 1:30 a.m.; after searching her house and taking her son's computer, she was detained in an undisclosed place for around 8–10 months, without any charge. Even though she was released, she still has to report to the local police regularly, and has to get approval even to visit our parents.

On the same day, August 17, 2014, RFA journalist Shohret Hoshur's two brothers were detained, and were later sentenced. This was obvious retaliation against Mr. Hoshur, who revealed a great deal about Chinese police brutality against Uyghurs.

As we all know, prominent Uyghur leader, human rights champion, and World Uyghur Congress (WUC) president Mrs. Rebiya Kadeer has constantly been accused by the Chinese government of being an evil separatist; and her two sons were sentenced to jail as retaliation from the Chinese government.

The Chinese government pressured one of Mrs. Kadeer's imprisoned sons to condemn his mother, and to accuse Mrs. Kadeer of being an evil criminal. As normal, civilized human beings, we cannot imagine under what circumstances, and under what kind of pressure, a son was forced to condemn his dearest mother, accusing his own mother publicly of being a criminal!

Dolkun Isa, another prominent Uyghur human rights activist, and chair of the WUC executive committee, was recently preparing to attend a meeting held in Dharamsala, India. The Indian government, after issuing a visa to Mr. Isa, and under the Chinese government's pressure, cancelled the visa, denying Mr. Isa entry into India.

In late 2009, Mr. Isa, as a German citizen, was in immediate danger of being repatriated back to China when he tried to enter South Korea to attend a human rights conference. He was put in solitary confinement for more than three days, before the U.S. and European Union intervened.

The Chinese government has constantly tried to block all of Mr. Isa's political activities by claiming he is a wanted terrorist according to an Interpol red notice, baselessly accusing him of supporting and funding terrorists.

Recently, another friend of mine, a Uyghur who is a Norwegian citizen, called me and told me that his family members living in East Turkistan were being harassed by the Chinese government; some of his family members were brought to the police station and interrogated for several hours, and they were told to tell him to stop any activities supporting Uyghurs.

Of course, we all know about the Uyghur refugees who managed to get out of China; but unfortunately, they were sent back to China by some irresponsible countries when they were in the process of applying for UNHCR refugee status. Some of them were directly interrogated by Chinese police in other countries, and their family members were threatened. After they were repatriated, most of them disappeared, and some of them were given harsh sentences.

The story of Uyghurs facing the Chinese government's constant persecution, harassment, and threats goes on and on. Even Uyghurs who live overseas can't be spared from the inhuman political persecution of the Chinese government. The Chinese government's long arm keeps stretching longer and longer. It's obvious that if China isn't pressured to stop this kind of harassment, no one will be safe, regardless of where we live.

––––––––––

PREPARED STATEMENT OF SU YUTONG

MAY 24, 2016

My name is Su Yutong. I am a journalist and activist based in Germany. In June, 2010, after I made public the personal diary of former Chinese Premier Li Peng, my house was ransacked by the police and I was forced to leave China. In August that year, I became a journalist with the Chinese section of Deutsche Welle where I wrote and published nearly 1,500 articles, most of which were about human rights and political affairs in China. The human rights lawyers and activists I reported included Chen Guangcheng, Ilham Tohti, Gao Zhisheng and Gao Yu. All of this work annoyed the Chinese Communist Party (CCP). Its state-owned newspaper Global Times attacked me in an article in August, 2014, for "constantly criticizing and vilifying China."

Before I came to the United States to participate in this hearing, I was in contact with Chinese journalist Gao Yu and the family members of detained human rights lawyers. Gao, aged 72, had already been jailed twice. She was arrested and sentenced to prison in April, 2014, for a third time, on charges evidently fabricated by the Chinese Communist Party. The real reason for her imprisonment was retaliation for an article she published in her Deutsche Welle column "Beijing Observer" which criticized Xi Jinping. I was her executive editor at the time. Last November, after Gao Yu was released on medical parole, the University of Bonn hospital was preparing to provide comprehensive treatment for her. And the German Ambassador to China issued her a visa to Germany. But the CCP authorities prevented Gao from leaving China for her medical treatment and ordered she remain silent.

Since July 9th, 2015, the Chinese government has been conducting a sweeping crackdown on human rights lawyers and activists. The wives of several detained lawyers asked me to bring two videos to this hearing. To this day, these women have been unable to visit their husbands in custody. No one knows what abuses these incarcerated lawyers and activists have been suffering. These women are appealing again to the international community for assistance. (I would like to request to show these two video clips at the hearing.)

At this hearing today, there is not enough time to tell the stories of all the human rights activists in China. Since Xi Jinping took power, China's human rights conditions have worsened constantly. The most courageous and outstanding people in China today are now in prison or on the way to prison. I am hoping such a human rights disaster will receive more media coverage and more attention from the international community. But there's one dangerous trend, that is how the CCP has reached its arms of news control overseas, as part of its "Great Overseas Propaganda Strategy." Such strategies include cross-border censorship and infiltration, attempting to muzzle international media in their coverage of China's worsening human rights conditions. As a journalist, I urge the Congress to pay more attention to this reality.

In 2011, Li Congjun, the head of Xinhua News Agency, described in a article in the Wall Street Journal the "new global media order". Hundreds of Confucius Institutes proliferate around the world as an important part of China's overseas propaganda campaign. The Chinese government has been pouring large amount of money in buying up overseas newspapers and radio networks. Benjamin Ismail, Asia Director of Reporters Without Borders (RSF) says RSF found a number of digital radio stations in Paris that had been secretly run by proxy companies operated by the Chinese government. In November, 2015, Reuters also reported that WCRW, a radio station based in Washington, D.C., has China International Radio, a Communist Party mouthpiece, as its hidden major shareholder. The radio waves of this station cover the entire Washington, D.C. region, including the Capitol Hill and the White House.

According to an investigation by Reuters, there are already 33 radio stations around that world that are affiliated with China International Radio. Numerous media outlets with the Chinese government as the controlling shareholder scatter throughout the world. And they hire local workers. At the press conferences during the annual sessions of National People's Congress and Chinese People's Political Consultative Conference in Beijing, CCP officials invited reporters from fake overseas media to ask pre-arranged, non-sensitive questions.

Buying off and cracking down—these are the two tactics being adopted in Hong Kong, once a paradise for books banned in China. Hong Kong publisher Yiu Mantin was sentenced to 10 years' imprisonment in China for publishing the book "Xi Jinping, China's Godfather." In March, relatives of New York-based activist Wen Yunchao (also known as Bei Feng) and German-based political commentator Chang Ping were detained and interrogated in relation to an open letter calling on Xi Jinping to resign.

Under the CCP's media control, a number of overseas and online Chinese-language media outlets have been serving as platforms to learn about a real China. When I was young, I secretly listened to Voice of America which is was and is still banned in China. These media outlets have now become targets of the CCP's incessant efforts at control. Chinese embassies and consulates around the world have started to play the role of the Ministry of Propaganda.

In 2013, my former employer Deutsche Welle hired Peter Limbourg as its new director. Soon after he assumed the post, Mr. Limbourg paid a visit to the Chinese division and told the staff that he had met with Shi Mingde, China's Ambassador to Germany. Mr. Limbourg demanded that the Chinese division not always criticize the Chinese authorities and should "appropriately encourage" them instead. In 2014, Mr. Limbourg hired Frank Sieren, a German businessman who is a long-term resident of Beijing. Mr. Sieren has had numerous business cooperations with the CCP's mouthpieces Global Times and China Central Television. In September, 2014, German newspaper Süddeutsche Zeitung reported the minutes of an April meeting between Deutsche Welle and China's Ambassador to Germany, which clearly revealed that the Chinese Embassy demanded Deutsche Welle change.

On June 4, 2014, Frank Sieren published an article in Deutsche Welle, in German and Chinese languages, describing Tiananmen Massacre as "a slip-up by the CCP." The piece sparked a public outcry from a number of pro-democracy activists and massacre survivors. I was a signatory to an open letter protesting this article. I spoke up against the article on Twitter. Soon afterwards, the deputy director and the director of the Deutsche Welle Chinese division, both of whom were highly critical of Mr. Sieren's article, were shifted to other positions. Meanwhile, I was fired by Deutsche Welle.

In late August, 2014, Mr. Limbourg traveled to Beijing to attend a Chinese-German media symposium hosted by CCP mouthpiece Global Times. At the same time, I published an open letter to him in the New York Times saying that "the voice of China" is currently attempting to use economic seduction and coercion to expand its "great overseas propaganda" campaigns around the world. My wishful thinking was that Mr. Limbourg, under the warm reception of Global Times, would not be drowned in Chinese wine and succumbed to become a tool in the CCP's "overseas propaganda campaigns." Much to my regret, Mr. Limbourg met with Wang Gengnian, the head of China Radio International, in Beijing on August 28, 2014. Mr. Limbourg said that Deutsche Welle's coverage would fit into the guidance and direction set by China. Soon afterwards, he announced a cooperative framework between Deutsche Welle and China Central Television (CCTV). In early 2015, Germany's Bundestag took note of this cooperation program and conducted a hearing. Deutsche Welle announced that it would temporarily suspend its cooperation with CCTV.

Meanwhile, Frank Sieren continues to write a column for Deutsche Welle. In 2008, another scandal took place at Deutsche Welle, when a DW reporter named Zhang Danhong lied on a German TV program that the human rights conditions in China were excellent. She was moved to another division at DW after protests. But in early 2015, Ms. Zhang was quietly returned to the Chinese department of DW, and was given her own column. All of these changes are sending subtle signals.

The CCP has been continuously expanding its scope of censorship. On May 10th, German legislator Michael Brand told the media that he was denied entry to China because of his criticism of China's Tibet policy. Mr. Brand, Chairman of the Committee on Human Rights and Humanitarian Aid of the German Bundestag, said the Chinese Embassy in Germany sent people to meet with him in person, demanding him delete his articles on Tibet from his official website. They also demanded Mr. Brand not to attend a meeting with a Tibetan human rights organization. Mr. Brand said such behaviors by the Chinese Communist Party are blatant and absurd, and it's unacceptable that the CCP exports its censorship to Germany.

Mr. Brand's stance is very clear and of great importance. We hope politicians in countries throughout the world dare to say "no" to the CCP. In recent years, as China has achieved economic progress, numerous countries choose silence and compromise on China's human rights abuses in exchange for contracts with the Chinese government. The most notable is the U.S. President Barack Obama who has been very weak and compromising when facing China's human rights issues. The Chinese government nowadays dares to reach its long arms to control the world, one factor is the brutal politics since Xi Jinping took power. The other reason is the appeasement from a number of countries.

As a media worker, I urge democratic countries to take notice of CCP's propaganda campaigns overseas, and its infiltration and disturbance of the freedom of press. The United States and other countries should organize investigations into China's infiltration of press freedom and media outlets established by the CCP; As a human rights activist, I am here to criticize and expose the increased crackdowns and persecution of human rights activists by the Chinese Communist government, especially under Xi Jinping's regime; I hereby request democratic governments not to neglect human rights conditions in China. Former U.S. President John F. Kennedy said his speech at West Berlin's Schöneberg Rathaus (City Hall) in 1963: "Freedom is indivisible, and when one man is enslaved, all are not free."

Finally, please allow me to express my gratitude to CECC's continuous focus on China's human rights conditions and assistance to activists all along. My special thanks go to Congressman Chris Smith and Senator Marco Rubio.

———

PREPARED STATEMENT OF HON. CHRISTOPHER H. SMITH, A U.S. REPRESENTATIVE FROM NEW JERSEY; CHAIRMAN, CONGRESSIONAL-EXECUTIVE COMMISSION ON CHINA

MAY 24, 2016

One year ago, Major Xiong Yan was barred from visiting his dying mother in China. He was repeatedly denied access to Mainland China because he is blacklisted, denied access to China because he was a student leader of the democracy protests of 1989. Tragically, Major Yan's mother passed away, her son never had the chance to say goodbye.

The Communist leaders in Beijing use the blacklist—along with intimidation, repression, and the lure of the Chinese market—to stifle discussion of the Tiananmen protests and their violent suppression.

Academics such as Perry Link and Andrew Nathan are also blacklisted for writing about Tiananmen. U.S. corporations, eager to gain access to the China's markets, also engage in censorship about Tiananmen. Last year the California based LinkedIn began blocking Tiananmen-related articles posted inside China or by members hosted on its Chinese site.

The methods used by Beijing to enforce a code of silence are going global. The heavy hand of the Chinese government has expanded beyond its borders to intimidate and stifle critical discussion of the Chinese government's human rights record and repressive policies.

Before I talk more broadly about our hearing today, let me first say a few words about the Tiananmen massacre.

The CECC has solemnly commemorated the Tiananmen massacre on and around June 4 each year. The Congress does this because of the lives lost and persons permanently injured in the massacre. We commemorate June 4th each year because of the profound impact the event has had on U.S.-China relations and because so many former student leaders have made important contributions to the global understanding of China. We mark the Tiananmen massacre each year because the Chinese people are unable to commemorate this event themselves.

This year the Congress is not in session on June 4th, but Senator Rubio and I will be sending a letter to President Xi Jinping asking him to allow uncensored, public discussion of the democracy protests of 1989; to end retaliation efforts against those who participated in the protests, and to release all those still detained for holding commemorations about the Tiananmen protests and their violent suppression.

We will urge President Xi to allow discussion of China's past history. We believe transparency is in the best interest of U.S.-China relations and will improve global perceptions of China.

Nevertheless, President Xi seems to have a different conception of what is in China's interest. As is well-documented already by this Commission, his government is engaged in an extraordinary assault on civil society and human rights. China is not only interested in containing the spread of "Western values and ideas" within China, but is actively engaged in trying to roll back democracy and human rights norms globally.

In fact it would be fitting to have an empty chair at the witness table today representing every dissident fearful of sharing their story, every writer whose work has been censored or edited by Chinese authorities without their knowledge and every journalist whose critical reporting has been blocked or tempered—not just in China, but in the West.

China's recent efforts to blunt scrutiny of its rights record and criticism of government policies include:

(1) Pressing Thailand and Cambodia to repatriate Uyghur refugees and Chinese asylum seekers.

(2) Disappearing and allegedly abducting five Hong Kong booksellers, including Gui Minhai, the father of one of our witnesses today.

(3) Supporting clandestine efforts to discredit the Dalai Lama through a Communist Party-supported rival Buddhist sect;

(4) Harassing and detaining the family members of foreign journalists and human rights advocates. Two of our witnesses today will attest to such harassment.

(5) Threating the operations of non-governmental organizations working in China through the newly passed Overseas NGO Management Law and other means. Dr. Teng Biao will talk about the cancelation of his book project by the American Bar Association.

We asked the ABA [American Bar Association] to testify today, but the ABA President Paulette Brown and the ABA's CEO Jack Rives were unable to testify. The ABA sent a letter to the Commission last month, responding to our inquiry about the details surrounding the ABA's rescinding of Teng Biao's book project. They want that letter to serve as their testimony.

A copy of the Commission letter to the ABA and the ABA's response will be added to the record without objection.

The long reach of China extends beyond its borders to Thailand, South Korea, Malaysia, India, Kenya, at the United Nations, and in the United States.

These efforts present real strategic implications for the United States and the international community. The abductions of the booksellers challenges the one-country, two systems model in Hong Kong. China's efforts to bend international human rights norms present a clear challenge to the United Nations and the Human Rights Council efforts to hold China accountable. China's efforts to enforce a code of silence globally through its economic and diplomatic clout directly challenges the Obama Administration's "Asia Pivot" and U.S. human rights diplomacy.

The President and his Administration have only a few more chances to raise human rights concerns with China. The Strategic and Economic Dialogue in two weeks and the G–20 meeting in September.

The Congress and this Commission will press the Administration to do more to advance human rights in China. President Obama must "shine a light" on human rights problems in China, because nothing good happens in the dark.

But we must also look ahead; use our Commission hearings, our Annual Report, and other publications to make a compelling case for the next Administration about the centrality of human rights to U.S. interests in Asia.

It is increasingly clear that there is direct link between China's domestic human rights problems and the security and prosperity of the United States. The health of the U.S. economy and environment, the safety of our food and drug supplies, the security of our investments and personal information in cyberspace, and the stability of the Pacific region will depend on China complying with international law, allowing the free flow of news and information, complying with its WTO obligations, and protecting the basic rights of Chinese citizens, including the fundamental freedoms of religion, expression, assembly, and association.

Losing sight of these facts leads to bad policy, bad diplomacy, and the needless juxtaposition of values and interests. It also sends the wrong message to those in China standing courageously for greater freedoms, human rights, and the rule of law. The human rights lawyers, the free press advocates, and those fighting for labor rights, religious freedom, and democracy are the best hope for China's future.

And, they are the best hope for a more stable and prosperous U.S.-China relationship.

———

PREPARED STATEMENT OF HON. MARCO RUBIO, A U.S. SENATOR FROM FLORIDA; COCHAIRMAN, CONGRESSIONAL-EXECUTIVE COMMISSION ON CHINA

MAY 24, 2016

Next week marks the 27th anniversary of the student-led popular protests in Tiananmen Square. Spurred by the death of a prominent reformer, thousands gathered in April 1989 seeking greater political freedom. Their numbers swelled as the days passed, not only in Beijing but in cities and universities across the nation. Eventually more than a million people, including journalists, workers, government employees and police, joined their ranks making it the largest political protest in the history of communist China.

Late in the evening of June 3, the Army opened fire on peaceful protesters. The bloodshed continued into June 4. To this day the precise number of resulting casualties is unknown and more than a quarter-century later there has been no progress toward a public accounting of the events of that week.

Instead, twenty-seven years later the Chinese government is increasingly brazen in its repression . . . no longer limiting its reach to China's territorial boundaries, but instead seeking to stifle discussion of its deplorable human rights record both at home *and abroad.* Consider the following:

Dissidents regularly report that their family members who remain in China are harassed, detained and even imprisoned in retaliation for their truth-telling about the regime's abuses.

News reports abound of Uyghur Muslim and Chinese asylum-seekers being forcibly repatriated from neighboring South Asian countries under pressure from the Chinese government.

Journalists and academics alike are threatened with visa revocations, thereby allowing self-censorship to take root in what should be the very bastions of free expression and inquiry.

Even educational institutions based in the United States are not immune as more have welcomed the establishment of Confucius Institutes. While seemingly benign at face value, the financial support that accompanies these centers for Chinese language and cultural education come with definite strings attached. Sensitive topics, including Taiwan and Tibet, are excluded from the curriculum, and invitations for the Dalai Lama to speak at prominent universities are mysteriously withdrawn.

In 2014, the American Association of University Professors issued a statement calling on colleagues across the United States and Canada to reconsider their partnerships with these centers, stating that, "Confucius Institutes function as an arm of the Chinese state and are allowed to ignore academic freedom."

In April 2016, the Indian government blocked several rights advocates and activists from attending an Interfaith/Interethnic Conference in Dharamsala, India reportedly due to Chinese government pressure to rescind their visas.

Last month, a news story broke alleging that the American Bar Association (ABA) had cancelled a proposed book project with prominent Chinese human rights lawyer Teng Biao, who we will hear from today. Multiple news sources reported that the project was canceled because of fears that the initiative would offend the Chinese government. The ABA denied these reports, claiming that the staff person in question who had interfaced with Teng Biao had been misinformed. Yet questions remain not only about the specifics of the book project but more broadly about the ability of groups like the ABA to continue working in China without compromising its principles.

And of course, any discussion of the "long arm" of Beijing must include recent troubling developments in Hong Kong, specifically the disappearances and alleged abductions of five Hong Kong booksellers, which have rightly raised alarm bells among Hong Kong activists, human rights organizations and foreign governments. The Commission will have the distinct privilege today to hear from Angela Gui, the daughter of missing bookseller Gui Minhai, a naturalized Swedish citizen who disappeared in October 2015 from Pattaya, Thailand. In the recent State Department Hong Kong Policy Act report to Congress, the Department rightly noted that, "These cases have raised serious concerns in Hong Kong and represent what appears to be the most significant breach of the 'one country, two systems' policy since 1997."

In a sad testament to the timeliness and importance of today's hearing topic, some of the witnesses the Commission approached with an invitation to testify declined based on very legitimate fears about what would happen to members of their family who remain in China. This is an inexcusable reality.

For too long, China has gotten a free pass. The Obama Administration's final U.S.-China Strategic and Economic Dialogue is just days away in Beijing. Will these issues be prioritized? Will every participating U.S. government agency be charged with bringing human rights to the forefront with their Chinese counterparts? Will there be consequences for China's bold and aggressive disregard for human rights and extraterritorial reach? In March, the United States spearheaded a collective statement at the U.N. Human Rights Council voicing serious concern about a number of issues to include the ''unexplained recent disappearances and apparent coerced returns'' of Chinese citizens and foreigners to China. The upcoming S&ED will be a litmus test for this Administration—the statement was commendable, but will words translate into action?

SUBMISSIONS FOR THE RECORD

STATEMENT SUBMITTED FOR THE RECORD BY WEN YUNCHAO

MAY 24, 2016

Honorable Representative Christopher Smith, Senator Marco Rubio, and CECC:

I, Wen Yunchao, hereby solemnly declare that the following narrative and news coverage about me and my family are true facts.

I arrived in the United States on December 27th, 2012. I lodged my application for political asylum in July, 2013. I have been waiting for the decision on my application. During this period, I have been subjected to tremendous pressure and harassment from the Chinese government.

In March 2016, the Chinese government suspected I was related to the publication and distribution of an "Open Letter Calling on Comrade Xi Jinping to Resign from All Party and State Leadership Positions." My parents and other family members and the family members of my wife Liu Yang in Guangdong were harassed, blackmailed, and threatened numerous times and were forced to disappear. My parents and brother were taken away by authorities on March 22nd and were released a week later. My wife Liu Yang's parents, brother and sister-in-law have been barred by the Chinese government from leaving China. Her parents had to cancel their plan to visit the United States in April. Liu Yang's brother and his wife have been subjected to disturbances in their daily work and life.

The facts in the following report by New York Times about me and the forced disappearance of my relatives in China are all true.

Wen Yunchao, a Chinese activist living in New York, said in a telephone interview that his parents and younger brother in southern China had been missing since Tuesday (Mar. 22, 2016), after police officers and officials warned his parents that Mr. Wen should tell them what he knew about the letter. Mr. Wen said he had nothing to do with distributing the letter on the Internet, and so refused to bow to the demands.

The letter, signed by "Loyal Communist Party Members," was sent by email to people with ties to China around the time it appeared on Wujie, shortly after 12:01 a.m. on March 4.

On Twitter, Mr. Wen, the activist, urged President Obama to ask Mr. Xi to release his parents and brother. "He kidnapped them on March 22," Mr. Wen wrote. Mr. Xi is expected to visit the United States next week for a summit meeting on nuclear security.

Mr. Wen said in the interview that his sister-in-law had told him that his parents and his younger brother, Wen Yun'ao, a driver for a local government, were all missing. Mr. Wen said his sister-in-law had given no details of when or how his parents disappeared but had said Wen Yun'ao, her husband, was taken away by officials.

Starting this month, Mr. Wen said, the police and officials repeatedly visited his father, Wen Shaogan, 71, and mother, Qiu Xiaohua, 64, at their home in Jiexi County, Guangdong Province, and told them that Mr. Wen had to admit to helping spread the letter.

"At the start, they said they wanted to know if I had anything to do with the open letter calling for Xi Jinping to resign," Mr. Wen said. "But on the 17th (Mar 2016), they said directly that they knew I hadn't written the letter but believed I had something to do with spreading it. They promised that if I told them who wrote the letter and passed it on to me, and how I spread it around, then I would not be held culpable and it would not be held against my family. Otherwise, they said, my younger brother might lose his job."

Mr. Wen, a vocal critic of the Chinese government who is also known by the pen name Bei Feng, said he had passed on a message to the officials through his parents that he had nothing to do with writing or distributing the letter.

"I told them very clearly that I could not admit to something that had nothing to do with me," Mr. Wen said. "I told them very clearly that I didn't write the letter and had not helped anyone to distribute it, and I had not issued the letter on any websites." (The New York Times: China Said to Detain Several Over Letter Criticizing Xi, By EDWARD WONG and CHRIS BUCKLEY, Mar. 25, 2016)

Please see below a report by AFP about me and the release of my relatives after they were forced to disappear. The facts in the article are all true.

Two overseas dissidents said on Wednesday (March 30) that Chinese police had released family members they claimed were detained as part of an official probe into a letter calling on President Xi Jinping to resign.

Wen told AFP that his father, mother and brother had been released after being held in the southern city of Guangzhou in southern Guangdong province.

The three were not charged with any crime and security officials accompanied them to tourist sites during their detention, he added.

"I think my family's release is related to Xi Jinping's visit to the US," he said, referring to the Chinese President's participation in a Washington summit this week.

Wen earlier claimed that his father warned before his detention that officials in Guangdong believed the exiled activist had "helped spread" the letter. (AFP: Dissidents say China relatives released in letter probe, Mar. 30, 2016)

Around the anniversary of the Tiananmen Massacre in 2015 and during the annual sessions of China's National People's Congress and the Chinese People's Political Consultative Conference in March 2016, my New York home's WiFi network was under DDOA attacks. I was unable to use the Internet properly. Days before the 25th anniversary of the Tiananmen Massacre in 2014, and just before Xi Jinping visited the U.S. in September, 2015, a number of Chinese government officials harassed my parents in Guangdong. They warned me not to criticize the Chinese government, especially not to criticize Xi and the Chinese economy.

Furthermore, I have been a frequent target of systematic online attacks and harassing phone calls since I left China in 2010. I believe these attacks are related to the Chinese government. For details, please refer to my testimony on June 25th, 2013, at the CECC hearing, "Chinese Hacking: Impact on Human Rights and Commercial Rule of Law."

Wen Yunchao

––––––––

TRANSCRIPTION OF VIDEO:
WORDS FROM WIVES OF HUMAN RIGHTS LAWYERS IN CHINA

Hello friends in the United States. We're wives of citizens and human rights lawyers who were arrested in the "July 9 Mass Arrests" in P.R. China. I'm Wang Qiaoling, wife of attorney Li Heping. I'm Yuan Shanshan, wife of attorney Xie Yanyi. I'm Li Wenzu, wife of attorney Wang Quanzhang. We feel very grateful to the international community and American friends for your persistent concerns about rule of law in China and the "July 9 incident."

During the process of "July 9 mass arrests," not only were the arrests illegal but also the homes and workplaces of all involved lawyers and citizens were searched illegally. Moreover, they were detained secretly in "residence under surveillance." Their family hired lawyers for them, yet their lawyers were barred from meeting them in person. Their lawyers were deprived of rights to meet and communicate with them.

After 6 months detention when the cases reached the state of "formal arrest," the family of each detainee received "Notification of Arrest," yet our loved ones were still deprived of their rights to meet and communicate with their lawyers. The Public Security authorities said that our loved ones have been assigned lawyers in the detention center, so the lawyers hired by us as family members were dismissed. But the lawyers hired by us want to have the chance to meet their clients to confirm the status of power of attorney, but they were also deprived illegally of their rights to meet their clients.

After the authorities locked up our loved ones illegally, they even put some requirements on us to obey their rules of "four not allowed": we're not allowed to hire lawyers by ourselves; we're not allowed to communicate with relatives of other detainees; we're not allowed to accept interview of media from abroad; we're not allowed to speak out on Internet. Facing these illegal and groundless requirements from the government we as family members didn't give in.

In the past 10 months, we worked together with our lawyers to stand fast in striving for our rights following legal procedures and insisted to speak out in public. After March 10, 2016, one statement from 12 countries to the United Nations about human rights situations in China, brought turning point to the "July 9 incident." After the publication of the statement from 12 countries to the UN on human rights situations of China, the situation of the "July 9 incident" began to change in China.

First of all, the prosecutor's office began to accept our letter of accusation. While before that, they rejected dozens of our letters of accusation [of illegal procedures]. The second part of the change was, the police officer handling this specific case tried to persuade each of us in private, requesting us as family members to accept the lawyers assigned by the government. The third part of the change was, in the previous two months Secret Police of China continuously approached the fellow countrymen in our hometowns, our old classmates and friends, our parents and elderships, the sisters and brothers of our loved ones, including us the wives of the detainees, and tried to get video recordings from us, and asked us to talk in front of the camera to persuade our detained family members to plead guilty. But to my delight, of course, all of us as family members held the same attitude and refused to do so. We requested the government to release our loved ones unconditionally.

During the whole course of the ''July 9 incident,'' public attention from the international society on this case pushed it toward the better ending. We owe thanks to all of you! We're also anxiously hoping our American friends continue to speak out and protest continuously without compromise in the days to come. Please unite with other Democratic countries to protest against the government of P.R. China. We also hope that the United States can use the chance of G–20 meeting as leverage to bring complete change to the ''July 9 incident.''

The Chinese officials take it as very important to be able to arrange private meetings with top leaders of Democratic countries. We hope that our American friends will request the Chinese officials to release people [in illegal detention] when they request private meeting [with the President of the United States]. Please ask the Chinese government to release all the citizens and lawyers detained in the ''July 9 incident'' for their human rights activities. We as family members of them admire one line in the national anthem of the United States, that is: ''the land of the free and the home of the brave.'' We hope our American friends in the land of the free and the home of the brave will give helping hands to rescue all the Chinese citizens and human rights lawyers that were detained in the ''July 9 incident.''

Thank you all!

LETTER FROM THE CONGRESSIONAL-EXECUTIVE COMMISSION ON
CHINA SUBMITTED TO THE AMERICAN BAR ASSOCIATION, APRIL 19,

April, 19, 2016

Paulette Brown   Jack L. Rives
President   Executive Director and Chief Operating Officer
American Bar Association   American Bar Association

Dear Ms. Brown and Mr. Rives,

We write to you as the chairs of the Congressional-Executive Commission on China (CECC) to
seek additional clarification about a recent report in *Foreign Policy (FP)* that the American Bar
Association (ABA) rescinded an offer to publish a book proposed by Chinese human rights lawyer
Teng Biao. We seek from you information to determine whether or not the book project was
canceled because of fears that ABA projects would be adversely affected in China or from actual
threats to ABA projects and partnerships in China. We invite you to respond in writing or by
submitting testimony to a CECC hearing next month that will examine the Chinese government's
global efforts to silence and punish its critics.

As a frequent witness before the CECC since his arrival in the United States in 2014, we have no
doubt that Teng Biao's proposed book would have offered an insightful window into the perils
facing China's legal professionals and rights advocates, something which the Commission
documented at length in its 2015 Annual Report. We are also deeply concerned about the
unrelenting pressures faced by Chinese civil society and foreign nongovernmental organizations
operating in China, particularly if the draft Overseas Nongovernmental Organizations (NGO)
Management Law is enacted in its current form.

We hope you can provide further clarification on both the pressures faced by the ABA from the
Chinese government that reportedly led to the cancellation of Teng Biao's book and the explanatory
statement made by Mr. Robert T. Rupp, Associate Executive Director for the Business Services
Group of the ABA, asserting that "the reasons resulting in the decision were miscommunicated to
Mr. Teng," and claims instead that "market research and sales forecasting conducted by the
association's publishing group," were the determining factors.

Many questions remain unanswered and we would be most grateful if you would provide
details to the following queries:

- Did the ABA receive any indication from the Chinese Government or any other
  individuals that the programs it facilitates in China would be jeopardized if, in
  fact, this book project was pursued?
- Do such calculations routinely enter in to ABA publishing decisions, either
  overtly, or indirectly?
- Was the ABA's decision regarding Mr. Teng's book influenced by concerns
  over the security and safety of ABA ROLI staff in China or potential
  retaliation against the partnerships and work of its commissions and
  individual members?

x   Did the ABA receive updated marketing information between December 2014, when the book was commissioned, and January 2015 when Teng Biao was notified of the offer being withdrawn?

As reported, the circumstances surrounding the cancellation of Teng Biao's book are deeply concerning and not worthy of the values and principles for which the ABA stands. Along with the inadequate statement made by the ABA last August in the wake of a major Chinese government crackdown on dozens of human rights lawyers, this latest incident seems to indicate that the ABA is unable to coordinate robust support for fellow legal professionals for fear of offending the Chinese Communist government. We look forward to your reply and welcome any additional information you are able to provide about this troubling case.

Sincerely,

Congressman Chris Smith   Senator Marco Rubio
Chair   Cochair

LETTER FROM THE AMERICAN BAR ASSOCIATION IN RESPONSE TO
LETTER FROM THE

AMERICAN BAR ASSOCIATION

1050 Connecticut Avenue, NW - Suite 400
Washington, DC 20036
(202) 662-1760
FAX: (202) 662-1762

April 25, 2016

The Honorable Chris Smith
Chair
Congressional-Executive Commission
  on China
243 Ford House Office Building
Washington, D.C. 20515

The Honorable Marco Rubio Co-
Chair
Congressional-Executive Commission
  on China
243 Ford House Office Building
Washington, D.C. 20515

Dear Representative Smith and Senator Rubio:

We are writing in response to your April 19, 2016 letter inquiring about the report that
the American Bar Association (ABA) rescinded a proposal to publish a book proposed
by Chinese human rights lawyer Teng Biao.

Let us begin by stating unequivocally that the publication decision was in no way related to ABA
programs or operations in China by the ABA Rule of Law Initiative (ABA ROLI) or other ABA
entities. The decision not to proceed with publication of the book was a business decision made
by the ABA Publishing Services Group after an assessment of projected book sales, including
advice from the ABA's retail distribution partner. None of the ABA ROLI staff knew about the
Teng book proposal until the ABA was contacted by the media earlier this month, some fifteen
months after the decision was made. ABA ROLI had no knowledge that the book was considered
for publication and ABA ROLI did not participate in any discussions about possible publication.
Moreover, there have never been any communications with the Chinese government about the
decision to publish this or any other book published or considered for publication by the ABA.
There would be absolutely no reason to do so.

Our responses to your specific questions follow:

- "Did the ABA receive any indication from the Chinese government or any other
  individuals that the programs it facilitates in China would be jeopardized if, in
  fact, this book project was pursued?" ANSWER: *None at all.*

- "Do such calculations routinely enter in to ABA publishing decisions, either
  overtly, or indirectly?" ANSWER: *They do not.*

- "Was the ABA's decision regarding Mr. Teng's book influenced by concerns
  over the security and safety of ABA ROLI staff in China or potential retaliation

42

against the partnerships and work of its commissions and individual members?"
ANSWER: *It was not.*

x   "Did the ABA receive updated marketing information between December 2014,
when the book was commissioned, and January 2015 when Teng Biao was
notified of the offer being withdrawn?" ANSWER: *The ABA never commissioned
the book or engaged in contract negotiations. No additional marketing
information was received after the end of November 2014.*

Before the end of November 2014, the ABA Publishing Services Group consulted with its retail
distribution partner about the viability of publishing Mr. Teng's book on the mass market. The
distributor projected that only 10% of the books would be sold and recommended against
publication of the book. Before receiving this reply, the ABA Publishing Services Group had not
finalized its decision on publishing the book but was disinclined to do so. The concerns voiced by
the ABA's retail distribution partner solidified the Publishing Group's decision to reject publication.

An ABA employee's initial communication to Mr. Teng of an offer to publish his book and that
employee's subsequent communication regarding the reasons for withdrawing that offer were
misguided as well as erroneous. The decision not to proceed with publication of Mr. Teng's book
was made for purely economic reasons; the reasons for the ABA's decision were unfortunately
miscommunicated to Mr. Teng.

The director of the ABA Publishing Services Group has publicly expressed his apologies for this
unfortunate miscommunication to Mr. Teng. We emphasize that discussions between Mr. Teng
and the Publications staff never reached the point of contract discussions, much less a signed
commitment. Further, Mr. Teng has certainly been free to pursue any and all other publication
venues for his book.

Your letter refers to "the inadequate statement made by the ABA last August in the wake of a
major Chinese government crackdown on dozens of human rights lawyers." We want to make
certain you are aware of several important actions the ABA has taken in support of the rule of law
and human rights in China.

On April 12, 2016, President Brown issued a call "for the Chinese government to protect human
rights under its own law and international law, heed the United Nations Basic Principles on the
Role of Lawyers, and observe fair trial and due process standards." This was the fourth public
statement of concern by an ABA President since last August. Last June, the ABA also submitted
detailed technical comments to the Chinese government on its Draft NGO Management Law.

In addition to these public statements, the ABA continues to be engaged in significant long-term
efforts in China. The ABA has worked tirelessly on the ground with Chinese NGOs, public
interest lawyers, universities, courts, and others to promote the rule of law and the protection of
basic rights for all citizens, including in the areas of LGBT rights, environmental rights, indigent
criminal defense, and protection of victims of domestic

violence. Through these and other efforts, the ABA has strongly supported initiatives that encourage the government of China to comply with its own laws and policies protecting rights, to develop such laws and policies where they do not exist, and to comply with international standards for the protection of human rights.

When visiting China in November 2015, President Brown emphasized the importance of the independence of the legal profession and the ability of lawyers to represent their clients without fear of reprisal. She raised this issue in private meetings and a public speech involving government officials and private sector lawyers. She also stressed the ABA's desire to expand its engagement in China to advance equal rights and the rule of law.

We are proud of our work in China and around the world to promote the rule of law and protect individual rights, and we appreciate the interest of the Congressional-Executive Commission on China in our efforts. Please feel free to add this letter to the record of your upcoming CECC hearing.

Sincerely,

Paulette Brown
President

Jack L. Rives
Executive

Original via U.S. Mail PDF
   copy via email to:
    Scott Flipse
    Director of Communications
    Scott.flipse@mail.house.gov

THE LONG ARM OF CHINA:
GLOBAL EFFORTS TO SILENCE CRITICS FROM TIANANMEN TO TODAY

MAY 24, 2016

Witness Biographies

Angela Gui, Student and Daughter of Disappeared Hong Kong Bookseller Gui Minhai

Angela Gui [rhymes with 'way'] is a 22-year-old final year undergraduate Sociology student at the University of Warwick, UK. As the daughter of Gui Minhai, she has followed and worked actively on his case with governments, police, and various human rights groups since his ''disappearance'' in October 2015. She also did a brief internship with his and Lee Bo's company Mighty Current Distributions in the summer of 2014. Aside from her studies and work on her father's case, Ms. Gui is also editor and creative director of Warwick Sociology Journal, an academic journal showcasing undergraduate and graduate student work from universities worldwide. After graduation Ms. Gui plans on continuing onto a master's degree in the History of Medicine, funded by the Wellcome Trust.

Ilshat Hassan, President of the Uyghur American Association

Ilshat Hassan is president of the Uyghur American Association. Born in Ghulja, in Xinjiang [pronounced SHEEN-JAHNG], he taught at a college in Shihezi [pronounced SURE-HUH-ZI] in Xinjiang for 15 years. In November 2003, his teaching career abruptly ended due to his political activities. He fled to Malaysia, leaving behind parents, a wife, and a teenage son. Mr. Hassan came to the United States as a refugee in July 2006, and soon after joined the Uyghur American Association, where he became a very active Uyghur human rights campaigner. He writes and blogs frequently in Chinese and is well known in the overseas Chinese democracy community.

Su Yutong, Journalist, Internet Activist, and Former News Broadcaster for the Chinese Service of Deutsche Welle

Su Yutong is a Chinese journalist and human rights defender. Because of her involvement in commemoration events linked to the Tiananmen massacre she was ''invited for tea'' and for ''chats'' by the Chinese authorities and kept under surveillance and periodically placed under house arrest. In 2010, after she distributed Li Peng's Diary, her home in China was raided and documents were confiscated by the police. After leaving China in 2010, she started working in Bonn with Deutsche Welle, the German international broadcaster. On July 4, 2014, a Beijing-based media consultant claimed in Deutsche Welle that some Western media were unfairly critical of the Chinese government crushing of the Tiananmen demonstrations—Ms. Su then became one of the most outspoken voices against this whitewashing of the 1989 events. In August 2014 Deutsche Welle ended their employment relationship.

Teng Biao, Chinese Human Rights Lawyer, Visiting Fellow at the Harvard Kennedy School and the U.S.-Asia Institute, NYU Law School, and Co-Founder of the Open Constitution Initiative

Dr. Teng Biao [rhymes with 'lung'] is a well-known human rights lawyer, Visiting Fellow at the Harvard Kennedy School and the U.S.-Asia Institute, NYU Law School, and the Co-founder of the Open Constitution Initiative. Dr. Teng Biao holds a Ph.D. from Peking University Law School and has been a visiting scholar at Yale Law School. He is interested in the research on human rights, judicial systems, constitutionalism, and social movements. As a human rights lawyer, Dr. Teng is a promoter of the Rights Defense Movement and a co-initiator of the New Citizens' Movement in China. In 2003, he was one of the ''Three Doctors of Law'' who complained to the National People's Congress about unconstitutional detentions of internal migrants. Since then, Dr. Teng has provided counsel in numerous other human rights cases, including those of Chen Guangcheng, rights defender Hu Jia [Who Jah], and many other religious freedom and death penalty cases.

www.ingramcontent.com/pod-product-compliance
Lightning Source LLC
Chambersburg PA
CBHW081756280526
45789CB00008B/2880